# Key *of* Heaven

Our God is one God in Three Persons, All our prayers are offered to the Blessed Trinity—usually to the Father, through the Son, in the Holy Spirit.

# Key *of* Heaven

## With Devotions, Inspiring Prayers, and Catholic Practices

*Edited by*
Rev. Francis Evans

***Illustrated***

CATHOLIC BOOK PUBLISHING CORP.
New Jersey

NIHIL OBSTAT: Rev. Pawel Tomczyk, Ph.D.
*Censor Librorum*

IMPRIMATUR: ✠ Kevin J. Sweeney, D.D.
*Bishop of Paterson*

January 31, 2023

The Nihil Obstat and Imprimatur are official declarations that a book or pamphlet is free of doctrinal or moral error. No implication is contained therein that those who have granted the Nihil Obstat and Imprimatur agree with the contents, opinions or statements expressed.



(T-908)

ISBN 978-1-947070-49-3



Printed in China 23 HA 1

catholicbookpublishing.com

# CONTENTS

## PART III: CATHOLIC PRAYERS



## PART IV: CATHOLIC DEVOTIONS

# INTRODUCTION

"PRAYER gives us strength for great ideals, for keeping up our faith, charity, purity, generosity; prayer gives us strength to rise up from indifference and guilt, if we have had the misfortune to give in to temptation and weakness. Prayer gives us light by which to see and to judge from God's perspective and from eternity. That is why you must not give up on praying!...

"In a conversation there are always an 'I' and a 'thou' or 'you.' In this case ... the 'Thou' is more important, because our prayer begins with God .... We begin to pray, believing that it is our own initiative that compels us to do so. Instead, we learn that it is always God's initiative within us...."

*Pope St. John Paul II*

As a sure means of deepening our faith in God and our love for Christ and His Church, this new edition of *Key of Heaven* contains a wide selection of inspiring prayers, devotions, Scripture, novenas, and blessings especially for the laity. A special effort has been made to include the official prayers of the Church and indulgences in accord with the most recent Pontifical Decrees.

Each prayer and devotion has its appropriate time and place. Men and women in all stations of life will, therefore, find in this modern prayer book complete prayers and devotions for any spiritual need. The "Prayers from the Bible" are taken from the popular and officially approved *New Catholic Bible.*

*Key of Heaven* has been edited with one thought in mind—that it may become an instrument for the greater glory of God and the salvation of souls. May it be the companion for all Catholics and produce abundant fruits for their salvation.

## Prayer before the Crucifix

Look down upon me, good and gentle Jesus
while before Your face I humbly kneel and,
with burning soul,
pray and beseech You
to fix deep in my heart lively sentiments
of faith, hope, and charity;
true contrition for my sins,
and a firm purpose of amendment.

While I contemplate,
with great love and tender pity,
Your five most precious wounds,
pondering over them within me
and calling to mind the words which David,
Your prophet, said to You, my Jesus:

"They have pierced My hands and My feet, they have numbered all My bones."
Amen.

# PART I
# CATHOLIC DOCTRINE

## –1–

## The Ten Commandments

1. I, the Lord, am your God. You shall not have other gods besides Me.
2. You shall not take the name of the Lord, your God, in vain.
3. Remember to keep holy the Sabbath day.
4. Honor your father and your mother.
5. You shall not kill.
6. You shall not commit adultery.
7. You shall not steal.
8. You shall not bear false witness against your neighbor.
9. You shall not covet your neighbor's wife.
10. You shall not covet your neighbor's goods.

## –2–

# The Seven Sacraments

JESUS is present among us today by means of the Sacraments. Through them Jesus acts in His Church and effects the salvation of all human beings. Sacraments are sensible signs, instituted by Christ to give us grace, which makes us children of God and heirs of heaven.

Our natural life follows a series of stages: we are born and grow until we become adults and can live on our own. In instituting the Seven Sacraments Jesus gave us helps to be born and grow to adulthood in the supernatural life—to be with us in every phase of life.

Baptism—Christ gives us a new life: the life of grace in His Church. We celebrate our birth to faith, as children of God, and we die to sin.

Confirmation—Christ strengthens us as Christians and He makes us His soldiers and apostles to defend and spread the faith.

Eucharist—We celebrate the Lord's Passover, the sacrifice of the Cross. Christ feeds us with the Bread of Life, His Body and Blood.

Reconciliation—Christ forgives our sins and restores or increases our grace. We celebrate our conversion and reconciliation with God and the Church.

Anointing of the Sick—Christ strengthens our soul in the face of sickness and death. We celebrate the Christian hope in life eternal.

Holy Orders—Christ consecrates His ministers for the Priestly Service of the People of God.

Matrimony—Christ sanctifies the indissoluble union of man and woman in mutual love and support, to have children and to bring them up in the Catholic faith.

## –3–

# The Precepts of the Church

## (Traditional Form)

1. To participate at Mass on all Sundays and Holydays of Obligation.
2. To fast and to abstain on the days appointed.
3. To confess our sins at least once a year.
4. To receive Holy Communion during Easter Time.
5. To contribute to the support of the Church.
6. To observe the laws of the Church concerning marriage.

## (Long Form)

FROM time to time the Church has listed certain specific duties of Catholics. Among those expected of Catholic Christians today are the following. (Those traditionally mentioned as Precepts of the Church are marked with an asterisk.)

1. To keep holy the day of the Lord's Resurrection: to worship God by participating in Mass every Sunday and Holyday of Obligation;* to avoid those activities that would hinder renewal of soul and body on the Sabbath (e.g., needless work and business activities, unnecessary shopping, etc.).

2. To lead a Sacramental life: to receive Holy Communion frequently and the Sacrament of Reconciliation regularly—minimally, to receive the Sacrament of Reconciliation at least once a year (annual confession is obligatory only if serious sin is involved);*—minimally also, to receive Holy Communion at least once a year, between the First Sunday of Lent and the Most Holy Trinity.*
3. To study Catholic teaching in preparation for the Sacrament of Confirmation, to be confirmed, and then to continue to study and advance the cause of Christ.
4. To observe the marriage laws of the Church;* to give religious training, by example and word, to one's children; to use parish schools and catechetical programs.
5. To strengthen and support the Church*—one's own parish community and parish priests, the worldwide Church and the Pope.
6. To do penance, including abstaining from meat and fasting from food on the appointed days.*
7. To join in the missionary spirit and apostolate of the Church.

## –4–

# Holydays of Obligation

## Holydays in the United States

Solemnity of Mary, the Holy Mother of God
*January 1*

Ascension of the Lord
*40 days after Easter or Seventh Sunday of Easter*

Assumption of the Blessed Virgin Mary
*August 15*

All Saints
*November 1*

Immaculate Conception of the Blessed Virgin Mary
*December 8*

Nativity of the Lord [Christmas]
*December 25*

## Holydays in the Church

HOLYDAYS of Obligation are special feasts for Catholics. Formerly there were many more, but the industrial age led to a curtailment of the number.

At the present time, there are ten Holydays of Obligation listed for the Universal Church, but each Episcopal Conference is free to reduce these in view of the circumstances of its particular country and people.

The ten include the six days listed above plus:

Epiphany of the Lord traditionally celebrated on January 6 but permanantly transferred to the first Sunday after January 1

Most Holy Body and Blood of Christ (Corpus Christi) permanently transferred to the Second Sunday after Pentecost

Solemnity of St. Joseph, Spouse of the Blessed Virgin Mary
*March 19*

Solemnity of Sts. Peter and Paul
*June 29*

## –5–

# Table of Moveable Feasts (2023-2033)

| Year of Our Lord | Ash Wednesday | Easter | Ascension | Pentecost | Most Holy Body & Blood | 1st Sun. Advent |
|---|---|---|---|---|---|---|
| 2023 | Feb 22 | Apr 9 | May 18 | May 28 | June 11 | Dec 3 |
| 2024 | Feb 14 | Mar 31 | May 9 | May 19 | June 2 | Dec 1 |
| 2025 | Mar 5 | Apr 20 | May 29 | June 8 | June 22 | Nov 30 |
| 2026 | Feb 18 | Apr 5 | May 14 | May 24 | June 7 | Nov 29 |
| 2027 | Feb 10 | Mar 28 | May 6 | May 16 | May 30 | Nov 28 |
| 2028 | Mar 1 | Apr 16 | May 25 | June 4 | June 18 | Dec 3 |
| 2029 | Feb 14 | Apr 1 | May 10 | May 20 | June 3 | Dec 2 |
| 2030 | Mar 6 | Apr 21 | May 30 | June 9 | June 23 | Dec 1 |
| 2031 | Feb 26 | Apr 13 | May 22 | June 1 | June 15 | Nov 30 |
| 2032 | Feb 11 | Mar 28 | May 6 | May 16 | May 30 | Nov 28 |
| 2033 | Mar 2 | Apr 17 | May 26 | June 5 | June 19 | Nov 27 |

## –6–

# Days of Fast and Abstinence

ON THE days of fast we must limit ourselves to one full meal. In addition to one full meal, two lighter meals are allowed. But snacking between meals breaks the fast and the precept.

The law of fast is binding on Catholics from age 18 to 59 inclusive. The sick (including pregnant women) are not bound by the precept. Other persons also may have sufficient grounds for being excused; e.g., if by fasting they cannot meet the demands of their regular work. In doubt, we may consult a priest, confessor, or any competent and trustworthy person.

In the United States, the days of fast prescribed by the Church are: Ash Wednesday and Good Friday.

On days of abstinence we must abstain from meat. The law of abstinence is binding on Catholics from age 14; there is no upper limit. Conditions of health, unavailability of meatless fare, etc., may excuse a person.

In the United States, Friday remains a day of penance and the tradition of abstinence from meat has primary place although an alternate penance or work of charity may be chosen.

By obligation, Ash Wednesday, Good Friday and all other Fridays of Lent are days of abstinence from meat.

While modifying the penitential practices of the past remembered by many older Catholics, the Church continues to teach the necessity of penance in the life of every Christian.

## –7–

# Indulgences

*FROM the Council of Trent to the beginning of Vatican II, many Catholics had a particular fondness for prayers that were indulgenced by the Church. Undoubtedly, they felt that in reciting such prayers they were guarded from praying fruitlessly, so to speak. However, the precise nature of indulgences often escaped the faithful and abuses crept into the practice, so that they came to be used by some in an almost magical way.*

*On January 1, 1967, Pope Paul VI promulgated new norms regarding the discipline of indulgences in the Church. The document dealt with the nature of sin, the punishment due to sin, the solidarity of all human beings in Adam and in Christ, the Communion of Saints, and the treasury of the expiations and merits of Christ, of the Blessed Virgin, and of the Saints—a treasury that has been given to the Church to be placed by her at the disposition of the faithful.*

*It also stressed how salutary is the use of indulgences, since they promote through charity the union of all the faithful with Christ and with the pastors of the Church, His representatives. At the same time it called for a revision of the indulgenced prayers and practices. This became a reality when a revised Latin edition of the* Enchiridion of Indulgences *was published in 1968 and an English edition in 1969. (A later Latin edition appeared in 1986 that was substantially the same as the previous edition, and its*

*1991 English equivalent was entitled* Handbook of Indulgences*).*

*The key idea of this new volume is the preeminent value of charity. The faithful are urged to look first of all to the worthy performance of their duties, with the assurance of obtaining not only greater merit but also a proportionate remission of temporal punishment for their sins already forgiven, this by virtue both of their personal effort and of the gift of the Church.*

*This section presents all the new indulgenced prayers and grants as well as many of the practices, so that the faithful can make use of them at opportune times and derive the greatest benefit from them. (It should always be remembered, however, that the Mass and the Sacraments remain the outstanding sources of sanctification and purification—no matter how good any such indulgenced works and patiently endured sufferings may be.)*

For the complete list of practices as well as a more complete treatment of *indulgences*, the reader is referred to the source of this entire section: the *Enchiridion of Indulgences*, authorized English edition, published 1969 by Catholic Book Publishing Corp. or the latest edition, the *Handbook of Indulgences*, published 1991 by the same firm.

## Introduction

1. AN INDULGENCE is the remission before God of the temporal punishment due for sins already forgiven as far as their guilt is concerned. This remission the faithful with the proper dispositions and under certain determined conditions acquire through the intervention of the Church which, as minister of

the Redemption, authoritatively dispenses and applies the treasury of the satisfaction won by Christ and the Saints.

2. An indulgence is partial or plenary, according as it removes either part or all of the temporal punishment due for sin.

3. No one, acquiring indulgences, can apply them to other living persons.

4. Partial as well as plenary indulgences can always be applied to the departed by way of suffrage.

5. The grant of a partial indulgence is designated only with the words "partial indulgence," without any determination of days or years.

6. The faithful, who at least with contrite heart perform an action to which a partial indulgence is attached, obtain, in addition to the remission of temporal punishment acquired by the action itself, an equal remission of punishment through the intervention of the Church.

7. The faithful, who devoutly use an article of devotion (crucifix or cross, rosary, scapular or medal) properly blessed by any priest, obtain a partial indulgence.

   But if the article of devotion has been blessed by the Pope or by any bishop, the faithful, using it devoutly, can also gain a plenary indulgence on the feast of the Holy Apostles, Peter and Paul, provided they also make a profession of faith according to any legitimate formula.

8. To be capable of gaining an indulgence for oneself, it is required that one be baptized, not excommunicated, in the state of grace at least at the completion of the prescribed works, and a subject of the one granting the indulgence.

9. In order that one who is capable may actually gain indulgences, one must have at least a general intention to gain them and must in accordance with the tenor of the grant perform the enjoined works at the time and in the manner prescribed.

10. A plenary indulgence can be acquired only once in the course of a day. But one can obtain the plenary indulgence for the moment of death, even if another plenary indulgence had already been acquired on the same day. A partial indulgence can be acquired more than once a day, unless otherwise expressly indicated.

11. The work prescribed for acquiring a plenary indulgence connected with a church or oratory consists in a devout visit and the recitation during the visit of one Our Father and the Creed.

12. To acquire a plenary indulgence it is necessary to perform the work to which the indulgence is attached and to fulfill the following three conditions: Sacramental Confession, Eucharistic Communion, and prayer for

the intention of the Sovereign Pontiff. It is further required that all attachment to sin, even venial sin, be absent.

13. The three conditions may be fulfilled several days before or after the performance of the prescribed work; it is, however, fitting that Communion be received and the prayer for the intention of the Sovereign Pontiff be said on the same day the work is performed.

14. A single Sacramental Confession suffices for gaining several plenary indulgences; but Communion must be received and prayer for the intention of the Sovereign Pontiff must be recited for the gaining of each plenary indulgence.

15. The condition of praying for the intention of the Sovereign Pontiff is fully satisfied by reciting one Our Father and one Hail Mary; nevertheless, each one is free to recite any other prayer according to his piety and devotion.

16. To gain an indulgence attached to a prayer, it is sufficient to recite the prayer alternately with a companion or to follow it mentally while it is being recited by another.

## First General Grant

A PARTIAL indulgence is granted to the faithful who, in the performance of their duties and in bearing the trials of life, raise their mind with humble confidence to God, adding—even if only mentally—some pious invocation.

This first grant is intended to serve as an incentive to the faithful to put into practice the commandment of Christ to "pray always and never lose heart" (Lk 18:1) and at the same time as a reminder so to perform their respective duties as to preserve and strengthen their union with Christ.

## Importunate Prayer

"Ask, and it will be given to you; seek,
and you will find;
knock, and the door will be opened to you.
For everyone who asks will receive,
and those who seek will find,
and to those who knock the door will be opened."

*Matthew 7:7-8*

*See also Matthew 26:41; Luke 21:34-36; Acts 2:42; Romans 12:12; Ephesians 6:18; Colossians 4:2; 1 Thessalonians 5:17-18.*

## Second General Grant

A PARTIAL indulgence is granted to the faithful, who in a spirit of faith and mercy give of themselves or of their goods to serve their neighbor in need.

This second grant is intended to serve as an incentive to the faithful to perform more frequent acts of charity and mercy, thus following the example and obeying the command of Christ Jesus (Jn 13:15; Acts 10:38).

However, not all works of charity are thus indulgenced, but only those which "serve their brothers and sisters in need," in need, for example, of food or clothing for the body or of instruction or comfort for the soul.

## Serving Christ in Others

"'For I was hungry and you gave me something to eat;
I was thirsty and you gave me something to drink;
I was a stranger and you welcomed me;
I was naked and you clothed me;
I was ill and you took care of me;
I was in prison and you came to visit me.'
"'Amen, I say to you,
whatever you did for one of the least
of these brethren of mine, you did for me.'"

*Matthew 25:35-36, 40*

*See also Tobit 4:7-8 and Isaiah 58:7.*

## Service of Others for Christ

MINDFUL of the Lord's saying:
"This is how everyone will know
that you are My disciples:
your love for one another" (Jn 13:35),
Christians cannot yearn for anything more ardently
than to serve the people of the modern world
with mounting generosity and success. . . .
Now the Father wills that in all human beings

we recognize Christ our Brother
and love Him effectively, in word and in deed.

Constitution on the Church in the Modern World, *no. 93.*
*See also* Decree on the Apostolate of the Laity, *nos. 8 and 31c.*

## Third General Grant

A PARTIAL indulgence is granted to the faithful, who in a spirit of penance voluntarily deprive themselves of what is licit and pleasing to them.

This third grant is intended to move the faithful to bridle their passions and thus learn to bring their bodies into subjection and to conform themselves to Christ in His poverty and suffering (see Mt 8:20 and 16:24).

But self-denial will be more precious, if it is united to charity, according to the teaching of St. Leo the Great: "Let us give to virtue what we refuse to self indulgence. Let what we deny ourselves by fast—be the refreshment of the poor."

## Following of Christ

"Anyone who wishes to follow me
must deny himself,
take up his cross daily,
and follow me." *Luke 9:23*

## Three Ways of Doing Penance

THE Church urges all the faithful
to live up to the Divine commandment of penance
by afflicting their bodies by some acts of chastisement,

over and above the discomforts and annoyances of everyday life. . . .
There are three principal ways
of satisfying the commandment to do penance,
handed down from ancient times—
prayer, fasting, and works of charity—
even though abstinence from meat and fasting have received special stress.

*Paul VI:* Apostolic Constitution on Penance, *no. III, e.*

*See also* Decree on Priestly Training, *no, 9, and* Dogmatic Constitution on the Church, *nos. 10 and 41.*

## –2–

## Other Grants of Indulgences

*THE individual works, described in the following pages, are each enriched with indulgences. The grant of a partial indulgence is sometimes expressly stated; very often, however, it is merely indicated by the words:* Partial indulgence.

For the complete list of grants, consult the *Enchiridion of Indulgences*, authorized English edition, published 1969 by Catholic Book Publishing Corp., or the latest edition, the *Handbook of Indulgences*, published 1991 by the same firm.

### Direct, We Beg You, O Lord

DIRECT, we beg You, O Lord,
our actions by Your holy inspirations,
and carry them on by Your gracious assistance,
that every prayer and work of ours may begin always with You,
and through You be happily ended. Amen.

*Partial indulgence.*

## Acts of the Theological Virtues and of Contrition

A partial indulgence *is granted to the faithful, who recite devoutly, according to any legitimate formula, the acts of the theological virtues (faith, hope, love) and of contrition. Each act is indulgenced.*

## Adoration of the Most Blessed Sacrament

A partial indulgence *is granted to the faithful, who visit the Most Blessed Sacrament to adore it; a plenary indulgence is granted, if the visit lasts for at least one half an hour.*

## Hidden God

HIDDEN God, devoutly I adore You,
Truly present underneath these veils:
All my heart subdues itself before You,
Since it all before You faints and fails.

Not to sight, or taste, or touch be credit,
Hearing only do we trust secure;
I believe, for God the Son has said it—
Word of Truth that ever shall endure.

On the Cross was veiled Your Godhead's splendor,
Here Your manhood lies hidden too;
Unto both alike my faith I render,
And, as sued the contrite thief, I sue.

Though I look not on Your wounds with Thomas,
You, my Lord, and You, my God, I call:
Make me more and more believe Your promise,
Hope in You, and love You over all.

O memorial of my Savior dying,
Living Bread, that gives life to man;

Make my soul, its life from You supplying,
Taste Your sweetness, as on earth it can.

Deign, O Jesus, Pelican of heaven,
Me, a sinner, in Your Blood to lave,
To a single drop of which is given
All the world from all its sin to save.

Contemplating, Lord, Your hidden presence,
Grant me what I thirst for and implore,
In the revelation of Your essence
To behold Your glory evermore.

*A* partial indulgence *is granted to the faithful, who recite devoutly the above hymn.*

## We Give You Thanks

WE GIVE You thanks, Almighty God,
for all your blessings:
Who live and reign for ever and ever. Amen.

*Partial indulgence.*

## Angel of God

ANGEL of God, my guardian dear,
to whom His love commits me here,
enlighten and guard,
rule and guide me. Amen.

*Partial indulgence.*

## The Angel of the Lord

a) *During the year* (outside of Easter Time)

℣. The Angel of the Lord declared unto Mary,

℟. *And she conceived of the Holy Spirit.*

*Hail Mary.*

℣. Behold the handmaid of the Lord,

℟. *Be it done unto me according to your word.*

*Hail Mary.*

℣. And the Word was made flesh,

℟. *And dwelt among us.*

*Hail Mary.*

℣. Pray for us, O holy Mother of God,

℟. *That we may be made worthy of the promises of Christ.*

Let us pray.
Pour forth, we beg You, O Lord,
Your grace into our hearts:
that we, to whom the Incarnation of Christ Your Son
was made known by the message of an Angel,
may by His Passion and Cross
be brought to the glory of His Resurrection.
Through the same Christ our Lord. Amen.

## Queen of Heaven

b) *During Easter Time*

QUEEN of Heaven, rejoice, alleluia:
For He Whom you merited to bear, alleluia,
Has risen, as He said, alleluia.
Pray for us to God, alleluia.

℣. Rejoice and be glad, O Virgin Mary, alleluia.

℟. *Because the Lord is truly risen, alleluia.*

Let us pray.
O God, Who by the Resurrection of Your Son,
our Lord Jesus Christ,
granted joy to the whole world:

grant, we beg You,
that through the intercession of the Virgin Mary,
His Mother,
we may lay hold of the joys of eternal life.
Through the same Christ our Lord. Amen.

*A partial indulgence is granted to the faithful, who devoutly recite the above prayers according to the formula indicated for the time of the year.*

*It is a praiseworthy practice to recite these prayers in the early morning, at noon, and in the evening.*

## Soul of Christ

SOUL of Christ, sanctify me.
Body of Christ, save me.
Blood of Christ, inebriate me
Water from the side of Christ, wash me.
Passion of Christ, strengthen me.
O good Jesus, hear me.
Within Your wounds, hide me.
Separated from You let me never be.
From the malignant enemy, defend me.
At the hour of death, call me.
To come to You, bid me,
That I may praise You in the company
Of Your Saints, for all eternity. Amen.

*Partial indulgence.*

## Papal Blessing

*A* plenary indulgence *is granted to the faithful, who piously and devoutly receive, even by radio transmission, the Blessing of the Sovereign Pontiff, when imparted to Rome and the World.*

## Act of Spiritual Communion

*An act of spiritual Communion, according to any pious formula, is enriched with a* partial indulgence.

## I Believe in God

*A* partial indulgence *is granted to the faithful, who piously recite the Apostles' Creed or the Nicene-Constantinopolitan Creed.*

## Out of the Depths

*A* partial indulgence *is granted to the faithful, who piously recite the psalm* Out of the depths (Psalm 130).

## Christian Doctrine

*A* partial indulgence *is granted to the faithful, who take part in teaching or in learning Christian doctrine.*

N.B.: *One who in a spirit of faith and charity teaches Christian doctrine can gain a partial indulgence according to the second of the three general grants of indulgences; see above.*

*This new grant confirms the partial indulgence in favor of the teacher of Christian doctrine and extends it to the learner.*

## Lord, God Almighty

LORD, God Almighty,
You have brought us safely to the beginning of this day.
Defend us today by Your mighty power,
that we may not fall into any sin,
but that all our words may so proceed

and all our thoughts and actions be so directed,
as to be always just in Your sight.
Through Christ our Lord. Amen.

*Partial indulgence.*

## Look Down Upon Me, Good and Gentle Jesus

LOOK down upon me,
good and gentle Jesus,
while before Your face I humbly kneel,
and with burning soul pray and beseech You
to fix deep in my heart
lively sentiments of faith, hope, and charity,
true contrition for my sins,
and a firm purpose of amendment,
while I contemplate with great love and tender pity
Your five wounds,
pondering over them within me,
calling to mind the words that David, Your Prophet,
said of You, my good Jesus:
"They have pierced My hands and My feet;
they have numbered all My bones" (Ps 22:17-18).

A plenary indulgence *is granted on each Friday of Lent to the faithful, who after Communion piously recite the above prayer before an image of Christ crucified; on other days of the year the indulgence is* partial.

## Eucharistic Congress

*A* plenary indulgence *is granted to the faithful, who devoutly participate in the customary solemn Eucharistic Rite at the close of a Eucharistic Congress.*

## Hear Us

HEAR us,
Lord, holy Father, almighty and eternal God;
and graciously send Your holy Angel from heaven
to watch over, to cherish, to protect,
to abide with, and to defend
all who dwell in this house.
Through Christ our Lord. Amen.

*Partial indulgence.*

## Spiritual Exercises

*A* plenary indulgence *is granted to the faithful, who spend at least three whole days in the spiritual exercises of a retreat.*

## The Moment of Death

*To the faithful in danger of death, who cannot be assisted by a priest to bring them the Sacraments and impart the Apostolic Blessing with its plenary indulgence, Holy Mother Church nevertheless grants a* plenary indulgence *to be acquired at the point of death, provided they are properly disposed and have been in the habit of reciting some prayers during their lifetime. The use of a crucifix or a cross to gain this indulgence is praiseworthy.*

*The condition: provided they* have been in the habit of reciting some prayers during their lifetime *supplies in such cases for the three usual conditions required for the gaining of a plenary indulgence.*

*The* plenary indulgence *at the point of death can be acquired by the faithful, even if they have already obtained another plenary indulgence on the same day.*

## Litanies

*The following Litanies are each enriched with a* partial indulgence: *the Most Holy Name of Jesus, the Most Sacred Heart of Jesus, the Most Precious Blood of our Lord Jesus Christ, the Blessed Virgin Mary, St. Joseph, and the Saints.*

## Magnificat

A partial indulgence *is granted to the faithful, who piously recite the canticle of the Magnificat.*

## Mary, Mother of Grace

MARY, Mother of grace,
Mother of mercy,
Shield me from the enemy
And receive me at the hour of my death.

*Partial indulgence.*

## Memorare

REMEMBER, O most gracious Virgin Mary,
that never was it known
that anyone who fled to your protection,
implored your help or sought your intercession,
was left unaided.
Inspired with this confidence,
I fly to you, O Virgin of virgins, my Mother;
to you do I come,

before you I stand, sinful and sorrowful.
O Mother of the Word Incarnate,
despise not my petitions,
but in your mercy hear and answer me. Amen.

*Partial indulgence.*

## Novena Devotions

*A* partial indulgence *is granted to the faithful, who devoutly take part in the pious exercises of a public novena before the feast of Christmas or Pentecost, or the Immaculate Conception of the Blessed Virgin Mary.*

## Use of Articles of Devotion

*The faithful, who devoutly use an article of devotion (crucifix or cross, rosary, scapular or medal) properly blessed by any priest, obtain a* partial indulgence.

*But if the* article of devotion *has been blessed by the Sovereign Pontiff or by any Bishop, the faithful, using it, can also gain a* plenary indulgence *on the feast of the Holy Apostles, Peter and Paul, provided they also make a profession of faith according to any legitimate formula.*

## Let Us Pray for Our Sovereign Pontiff

℣. Let us pray for our Sovereign Pontiff *N.*

℟. **The Lord preserve him and give him life, and make him blessed upon the earth, and deliver him not up to the will of his enemies.**

*Partial indulgence.*

## First Communion

A plenary indulgence *is granted to the faithful, when they receive Communion for the first time, or when they assist at the sacred ceremonies of a First Communion.*

## First Mass of Newly-Ordained Priests

A plenary indulgence *is granted to a priest on the occasion of the first Mass he celebrates with some solemnity and to the faithful who devoutly assist at the same Mass.*

## Monthly Recollection

A partial indulgence *is granted to the faithful, who take part in a monthly retreat.*

## Eternal Rest

ETERNAL rest grant to them,
O Lord,
and let perpetual light shine upon them.
May they rest in peace.

Partial indulgence, *applicable only to the souls in purgatory.*

## Reading of Sacred Scripture

A partial indulgence *is granted to the faithful, who with the veneration due the Divine Word make a spiritual reading from Sacred Scripture.* A plenary indulgence *is granted, if this reading is continued for at least one half an hour.*

## Hail, Holy Queen

HAIL, holy Queen, Mother of mercy;
hail, our life, our sweetness and our hope.

To you do we cry,
poor banished children of Eve.
To you do we send up our sighs,
mourning and weeping in this valley of tears.
Turn then, most gracious Advocate,
your eyes of mercy toward us.
And after this our exile
show unto us the blessed fruit of your womb, Jesus.
O clement, O loving, O sweet Virgin Mary.

*Partial indulgence.*

## Sign of the Cross

*A* partial indulgence *is granted to the faithful, who devoutly sign themselves with the Sign of the Cross, while saying the customary words.*

IN THE Name of the Father,
and of the Son,
and of the Holy Spirit. Amen.

## Te Deum

YOU are God: we praise You;
You are the Lord: we acclaim You;
You are the eternal Father:
All creation worships You.

To You all Angels, all the Powers of heaven,
Cherubim and Seraphim, sing in endless praise:
Holy, holy, holy, Lord, God of power and might,
heaven and earth are full of Your glory.

The glorious company of Apostles praise You.
The noble fellowship of Prophets praise You.

**The white-robed army of Martyrs praise You.**
**Throughout the world the holy Church acclaims You:**
**Father, of majesty unbounded,**
**Your true and only Son, worthy of all worship,**
**and the Holy Spirit, advocate and guide.**

**You, Christ, are the King of glory,**
**the eternal Son of the Father.**

**When You became Man to set us free**
**You did not spurn the Virgin's womb.**

**You overcame the sting of death,**
**and opened the Kingdom of Heaven to all believers.**

**You are seated at God's right hand in glory.**
**We believe that You will come, and be our Judge.**

**Come then, Lord, and help Your people,**
**bought with the price of Your own Blood,**
**and bring us with Your Saints**
**to glory everlasting.**

℣. Save Your people, Lord, and bless Your inheritance.
℟. **Govern and uphold them now and always.**
℣. Day by day we bless You.
℟. **We praise Your Name for ever.**
℣. Keep us today, Lord, from all sin.
℟. **Have mercy on us, Lord, have mercy.**
℣. Lord, show us Your love and mercy;
℟. **for we put our trust in You.**
℣. In You, Lord, is our hope:
℟. **and we shall never hope in vain.**

*A* partial indulgence *is granted to the faithful, who recite the* Te Deum *in thanksgiving. But a* plenary indulgence *is granted, if the hymn is recited publicly on the last day of the year.*

## Come, Holy Spirit

**COME, Holy Spirit,
fill the hearts of Your faithful
and kindle in them the fire of Your love.**

*Partial indulgence.*

## Exercise of the Way of the Cross

*A* plenary indulgence *is granted to the faithful, who make the pious exercise of the* Way of the Cross.

*In the pious exercise of the* Way of the Cross *we recall anew the sufferings that the Divine Redeemer endured while going from the praetorium of Pilate, where He was condemned to death, to the mount of Calvary, where He died on the Cross for our salvation.*

## Renewal of Baptismal Promises

*A* partial indulgence *is granted to the faithful, who renew their baptismal promises according to any formula in use; but a* plenary indulgence *is granted, if this is done in the celebration of the Paschal Vigil or on the anniversary of one's Baptism.*

**GLORY** be to the Father, and to the Son, and to the Holy Spirit. As is was in the beginning, is now, and will be forever. Amen.

# PART II
# TRADITIONAL CATHOLIC PRACTICES

## *–1–*

## The Six Sins against the Holy Spirit

1. Presumption of God's mercy
2. Despair
3. Denial of the known truth
4. Envy at another's spiritual good
5. Obstinacy in sin
6. Refusal to be repentant

## *–2–*

## Nine Ways of Being an Accessory to Another's Sin

1. By counsel
2. By command
3. By consent
4. By provocation
5. By praise or flattery
6. By concealment
7. By partaking
8. By silence
9. By defense of the evil done

*–3–*

## The Seven Capital Sins (chief sources of sin)

1. Pride
2. Covetousness
3. Lust
4. Anger
5. Gluttony
6. Envy
7. Sloth

*–4–*

## The Seven Gifts of the Holy Spirit

1. Wisdom
2. Understanding
3. Counsel
4. Fortitude
5. Knowledge
6. Piety
7. Fear of the Lord

–5–

## The Eight Beatitudes

1. Blessed are the poor in spirit, for theirs is the kingdom of heaven.
2. Blessed are those who mourn, for they will be comforted.
3. Blessed are the meek, for they will inherit the earth.
4. Blessed are those who hunger and thirst for justice, for they will have their fill.
5. Blessed are the merciful, for they will obtain mercy.
6. Blessed are the pure of heart, for they will see God.
7. Blessed are the peacemakers, for they will be called children of God.
8. Blessed are those who are persecuted in the cause of justice, for theirs is the Kingdom of heaven.

–6–

## Satisfying the Debt of Our Temporal Punishment

THE chief ways of satisfying the debt of our temporal punishment besides the penance imposed after confession are prayer, attending Mass, fasting, almsgiving, the works of mercy, the patient endurance of sufferings, and indulgences.

–7–

## The Spiritual Works of Mercy

1. To admonish the sinner (correct those who need it)
2. To instruct the ignorant (teach the ignorant)
3. To counsel the doubtful (give advice to those who need it)
4. To comfort the sorrowful (comfort those who suffer)
5. To bear wrongs patiently (be patient with others)
6. To forgive all injuries (forgive others who hurt you)
7. To pray for the living and the dead (pray for others)

–8–

## The Corporal Works of Mercy

1. To feed the hungry
2. To give drink to the thirsty
3. To clothe the naked
4. To visit the imprisoned
5. To shelter the homeless
6. To visit the sick
7. To bury the dead

## –9–

## Lay Baptism

IN CASE of necessity any person can baptize if that person has the intention of doing what the Church does and pours water on the candidate's head while saying: "I baptize you in the name of the Father, and of the Son, and of the Holy Spirit."

## –10–

## Counsels and Maxims

• Never pretend to be what you are not; it is impossible to conceal your inward emptiness and defects for a long time.

• The neglect of your daily duties to serve God better is not the will of God.

• One of your most efficacious means of pleasing God should be to perform every action as though it were the last of your life.

• The salvation of your soul is so important, that in order to procure it, you should expose not only your property, but your life if necessary, to save your soul.

• If you place your confidence in God, you may be certain that should the entire Universe arise against you, nothing contrary to the will of God will happen to You.

• You can make no better use of earthly goods than to employ them in charity; for by this means you make them return to God, who is their source.

• One of the marks of the true Church is a love for the crucifix. No sect has this love.

• Good habits are the soul's muscles; the more you use them the stronger they grow and the easier work becomes.

• If you will seek God, you will find Him. Also, the more you seek Him the more love and fear you will have of Him.

• Humility is a state of mind in which we get the grace to quit lying to ourselves.

• Charity is like the object-glass of, a telescope; the broader you make it here on earth, the farther you can see into heaven.

• Great souls are always loyally submissive, reverent, to what is over them; only small, mean souls are otherwise.

• There are many dirty roads in life; but, if you use your judgment, you may always be able to find a clean crossing.

• Although you should speak to everyone with politeness, do not praise them unless you think it proper to encourage a timid soul or engage them to persevere in good works.

• When God deprives you of your bodily strength He desires you to understand that He has chosen other instruments for the execution of His designs.

• To be satisfied with every state in which God places you, and never to abandon it, is the most excellent and useful virtue that you can practice.

• Your spirit of obedience consists not only in doing what you are directed, but in a continual disposition of doing whatever shall be commanded of you.

• God permits troubles and afflictions to come to you in order to exercise your patience, and to teach you sympathy for the misfortunes of others.

• You ought to give yourself entirely to the hands of God, and believe that His Providence disposes for our greater good everything that He wishes or permits to happen.

• You should make fraternal charity the soul of your virtues as it is the paradise of religious communities.

• If you believe you are the author of the good you have done, or flatter yourself, you will lose more than you will gain, even if the works are good and holy.

• Understand that before you can be elevated to a union with God, you must first descend into the depths of your miseries.

• You should fear the judgments of Christ and not discuss them as they are incomprehensible to human understanding.

• With a humble mind it is better for you to implore the glorious sufferings of the Saints than to be inquisitive and search into their secrets.

• God has written that if you cast down your crowns before God and adore Him, you will have life everlasting.

**Jesus Our Consoler — "Come to Me, all you who are weary and overburdened, and I will give you rest. . . . You will find rest for your souls"**
*Matthew 11:25f.*

# PART III
# CATHOLIC PRAYERS

## –1–

## Prayers Every Catholic Should Know

### The Sign of the Cross

IN THE name of the Father, and of the Son, ✠ and of the Holy Spirit. Amen.

### The Lord's Prayer

OUR Father, Who art in heaven, hallowed be Thy name; Thy kingdom come, Thy will be done on earth as it is in heaven. Give us this day our daily bread, and forgive us our trespasses, as we forgive those who trespass against us; and lead us not into temptation, but deliver us from evil. Amen.

### The Hail Mary

HAIL, Mary, full of grace! The Lord is with thee; blessed art thou among women, and blessed is the fruit of thy womb, Jesus. Holy Mary, Mother of God, pray for us sinners now and at the hour of our death. Amen.

## Glory Be to the Father

GLORY be to the Father, and to the Son, and to the Holy Spirit. As is was in the beginning, is now, and will be forever. Amen.

## The Apostles' Creed

I BELIEVE in God, the Father Almighty, Creator of heaven and earth; and in Jesus Christ, His only Son, Our Lord, Who was conceived by the Holy Spirit, born of the Virgin Mary, suffered under Pontius Pilate, was crucified, died and was buried; He descended into hell; on the third day He rose again from the dead; He ascended into heaven, and is seated at the right hand of God the Father Almighty; from there He will come to judge the living and the dead.

I believe in the Holy Spirit, the holy catholic Church, the communion of saints, the forgiveness of sins, the resurrection of the body, and life everlasting. Amen.

## The Confiteor

I CONFESS to almighty God and to you, my brothers and sisters, that I have greatly sinned, in my thoughts and in my words, in what I have done and in what I have failed to do, through my fault, through my fault, through my most grievous fault; therefore I ask blessed Mary ever-Virgin, all the Angels and Saints, and you, my brothers and sisters, to pray for me to the Lord our God.

May Almighty God have mercy on me, forgive me my sins, and bring me to everlasting life. Amen.

May the almighty and merciful Lord grant me pardon, absolution, and remission of all my sins. Amen.

## An Act of Faith

O MY God, I firmly believe that You are one God in three Divine Persons, Father, Son, and Holy Spirit; I believe that Your Divine Son became Man, and died for our sins, and that He will come to judge the living and the dead. I believe these and all the truths which the Holy Catholic Church teaches because You have revealed them, Who can neither deceive nor be deceived.

## An Act of Hope

O MY God, relying on Your almighty power and infinite mercy and promises, I hope to obtain pardon for my sins, the help of Your grace, and life everlasting, through the merits of Jesus Christ, my Lord and Redeemer.

## An Act of Love

O MY God, I love You above all things with my whole heart and soul, because You are all-good and worthy of all love. I love my neighbor as myself for the love of You. I forgive all who have injured me, and ask pardon of all whom I have injured.

## Act of Contrition

O MY God, I am heartily sorry for having offended You, and I detest all my sins because of Your just punishments, but most of all because they offend You, my God, Who are all-good and deserving of all my love. I firmly resolve, with the help of Your grace, to sin no more and to avoid the unnecessary occasions of sin. Amen.

## Prayer to the Holy Spirit

COME, Holy Spirit, fill the hearts of Your faithful and kindle in them the fire of Your love.

℣. Send forth Your Spirit, and they shall be created.
℟. And You shall renew the face of the earth.

*Let us pray.* O God, Who did instruct the hearts of the faithful by the light of the Holy Spirit: grant that, by the gift of the same Spirit, we may be always truly wise, and ever rejoice in His consolation. Through Christ our Lord. Amen.

## Act of Spiritual Communion

MY JESUS, I believe that You are in the Blessed Sacrament. I love You above all things, and I long for You in my soul. Since I cannot now receive You sacramentally, come at least spiritually into my heart.

I know You have already come. I embrace You and unite myself entirely to You; never permit me to be separated from You. Amen.

## Invocations

MAY the Holy Trinity be blessed.

GOD the Father, have mercy on me.

GOD the Son, have mercy on me.

O HEART of Jesus, I place my trust in You.

JESUS, meek and humble of Heart, make my heart like unto Thine.

MAY the most Blessed Sacrament be praised and adored forever.

GOD the Holy Spirit, have mercy on me.

HOLY Mary, pray for me.

HOLY QUEEN conceived without original sin, pray for us.

## Hail, Holy Queen

HAIL, Holy Queen, Mother of mercy, hail, our life, our sweetness, and our hope! To you do we cry, poor banished children of Eve! To you do we send up our sighs, mourning, and weeping in this vale of tears!

Turn then, most gracious advocate, your eyes of mercy toward us; and after this, our exile, show unto us the blessed fruit of your womb, Jesus! O clement, O loving, O sweet Virgin Mary!

## Blessing before Meals

BLESS us, O Lord, and these Your gifts, which we are about to receive from Your bounty, through Christ our Lord. Amen.

## Grace after Meals

WE GIVE You thanks for all Your benefits, O Almighty God, Who live and reign forever. Amen.

May the souls of the faithful departed, through the mercy of God, rest in peace. Amen.

## Anima Christi

Soul of Christ, sanctify me.
Body of Christ, save me.
Blood of Christ, inebriate me.
Water from the side of Christ, wash me.
Passion of Christ, strengthen me.
O good Jesus, hear me.
Within your wounds hide me.
Separated from you let me never be.
From the malignant enemy, defend me.
At the hour of death, call me.
And close to you bid me.
That with your saints I may be
Praising you, forever and ever. Amen.

*Partial indulgence.*

**–2–**

# Morning Prayers

## Offering to the Holy Trinity

MOST holy and adorable Trinity, one God in three Persons, I praise You and give You thanks for all the favors You have bestowed upon me. Your goodness has preserved me until now. I offer You my whole being and in particular all my thoughts, words and deeds, together with all the trials I may undergo this day.

Give them Your blessing. May Your Divine Love animate them and may they serve Your greater glory.

I make this morning offering in union with the Divine intentions of Jesus Christ Who offers himself daily in the holy Sacrifice of the Mass, and in union with Mary, His Virgin Mother and our Mother, who was always the faithful handmaid of the Lord.

Glory be to the Father, and to the Son, and to the Holy Spirit. Amen.

## For Divine Guidance through the Day

LORD, God Almighty, You have brought us safely to the beginning of this day. Defend us today by Your mighty power, that we may not fall into any sin, but that all our words may so proceed and all our thoughts and actions be so directed, as to be always just in your sight. Through Christ our Lord. Amen.

Direct, we beg You, O Lord, our actions by Your holy inspirations, and carry them on by Your gracious assistance, that every prayer and work of ours may begin always with You, and through You be happily ended. Amen.

## Morning Offering (1)

O MY God, I offer You all my prayers, works, and sufferings, in union with the Sacred Heart of Jesus, for the intentions for which He pleads and offers Himself in the Holy Sacrifice of the Mass, in thanksgiving for Your favors, in reparation for my offenses, and in humble supplication for my temporal and eternal welfare, for the conversion of sinners, and for the relief of the poor souls in purgatory.

I wish to gain all the indulgences attached to the prayers I shall say and to the good works I shall perform this day.

## Morning Offering (2)

O JESUS, through the Immaculate Heart of Mary, I offer You my prayers, works, joys and sufferings of this day for all the intentions of Your Sacred Heart, in union with the Holy Sacrifice of the Mass throughout the world, in reparation for my sins, for the intentions of all our associates and in particular for all the intentions of this month (*mention intention if known*).

## Prayer for God's Protection and Christ's Presence

AS I arise today,
may the strength of God pilot me,
the power of God uphold me,
the wisdom of God guide me.
May the eye of God look before me,
the ear of God hear me,
the word of God speak for me.
May the hand of God protect me,
the way of God lie before me,
the shield of God defend me,
the host of God save me.

May Christ shield me today . . .
Christ with me, Christ before me,
Christ behind me,
Christ in me, Christ beneath me,

Christ above me,
Christ on my right, Christ on my left,
Christ when I lie down, Christ when I sit,
Christ when I stand,
Christ in the heart of everyone who thinks of me,
Christ in the mouth of everyone who speaks of me,
Christ in every eye that sees me,
Christ in every ear that hears me.

*St. Patrick*

## Litany of the Most Holy Name

LORD, have mercy.
*Christ, have mercy.*
Lord, have mercy.
Jesus, hear us.
*Jesus, graciously hear us.*
God, the Father of Heaven,
*have mercy on us.**
God the Son, Redeemer of the world,
God, the Holy Spirit,
Holy Trinity, one God,
Jesus, Son of the living God,
Jesus, Splendor of the Father,
Jesus, Brightness of eternal Light,
Jesus, King of Glory,
Jesus, Sun of Justice,
Jesus, Son of the Virgin Mary,
Jesus, most amiable,
Jesus, most admirable,
Jesus, the mighty God,
Jesus, Father of the world to come,
Jesus, angel of great counsel,

* *Have mercy on us* is repeated after each invocation, down to *Jesus, Crown of all Saints.*

Jesus, most powerful,
Jesus, most patient,
Jesus, most obedient,
Jesus, meek and humble of heart,
Jesus, Lover of Chastity,
Jesus, our Lover,
Jesus, God of Peace,
Jesus, Author of Life,
Jesus, Model of Virtues,
Jesus, zealous for souls,
Jesus, our God,
Jesus, our Refuge,
Jesus, Father of the Poor,
Jesus, Treasure of the Faithful,
Jesus, good Shepherd,
Jesus, true Light,
Jesus, eternal Wisdom,
Jesus, infinite Goodness,
Jesus, our Way and our Life,
Jesus, joy of the Angels,
Jesus, King of the Patriarchs,
Jesus, Master of the Apostles,
Jesus, Teacher of the Evangelists,
Jesus, Strength of Martyrs,
Jesus, Light of Confessors,
Jesus, Purity of Virgins,
Jesus, Crown of all Saints,

Be merciful, *spare us, O Jesus*!
Be merciful, *graciously hear us, O Jesus.*
From all evil, *deliver us, O Jesus.***

** *Deliver us, O Jesus...*, down to *Through Your Glory.*

From all sin,
From Your wrath,
From the snares of the devil,
From the spirit of fornication,
From everlasting death,
From the neglect of Your inspirations,
Through the mystery of Your holy Incarnation,
Through Your Nativity,
Through Your Infancy,
Through Your most Divine Life,
Through Your Labors,
Through Your Agony and Passion,
Through Your Cross and Abandonment,
Through Your Sufferings,
Through Your Death and Burial,
Through Your Resurrection,
Through Your Ascension,
Through Your Institution of the Most Holy Eucharist,
Through Your Joys,
Through Your Glory,

Lamb of God, You take away the sins of the world; *spare us, O Jesus*!
Lamb of God, You take away the sins of the world; *graciously hear us, O Jesus*!
Lamb of God, You take away the sins of the world; *have mercy on us, O Jesus*!
℣. Jesus, hear us.
℟. *Jesus, graciously hear us.*

# –3–

# Prayers during the Day

## Midafternoon Prayer

O DIVINE Savior, I transport myself in spirit to Mount Calvary to ask pardon for my sins, for it was because of humankind's sins that You chose to offer Yourself in sacrifice. I thank You for Your extraordinary generosity, and I am also grateful to You for making me a child of Mary, Your Mother.

Blessed Mother, take me under your protection. St. John, you took Mary under your care.

Teach me true devotion to Mary, the Mother of God. May the Father, the Son, and the Holy Spirit be glorified in all places through the Immaculate Virgin Mary.

## Invocations

MAY the Holy Trinity be blessed.
Christ conquers!
Christ reigns!
Christ commands!

O HEART of Jesus,
burning with love for us,
inflame our hearts with love for You.

O HEART of Jesus,
I place my trust in You.

O HEART of Jesus,
all for You.

MOST Sacred Heart of Jesus,
have mercy on us.
Teach me to do Your will,
because You are my God. *Psalm 143:10*

MOST Sacred Heart of Jesus,
have mercy on us.

O LORD,
increase our faith. *Luke 17:5*

SWEET Heart of Mary,
be my salvation.

JESUS, meek and humble of heart,
make my heart like unto Thine.

MAY the Most Blessed Sacrament
be praised and adored forever.

PRAY for us, O Holy Mother of God,
that we may be made worthy of the promises of Christ.

FATHER, into Your hands
I commend my spirit. *Luke 23:46; see Psalm 31:6*

MERCIFUL Lord Jesus,
grant them everlasting peace.

QUEEN conceived without original sin,
pray for us.

HOLY Mother of God, Mary ever-Virgin,
intercede for us.

HOLY Mary, pray for us.
My Jesus, mercy.

# –4–

# Night Prayers

## Prayer to the Blessed Trinity

I ADORE You, my God, and I thank You for having created me, for having made me a Christian and preserved me this day. I love You with all my heart, and I am sorry for having sinned against You because You are infinite Love and infinite Goodness. Protect me during my rest and may Your love be always with me. Amen.

Eternal Father, I offer You the Precious Blood of Jesus Christ in atonement for my sins and for all the intentions of our Holy Church.

Holy Spirit, Love of the Father and the Son, purify my heart, and fill it with the fire of Your Love, so that I may be a chaste Temple of the Holy Trinity and be always pleasing to You in all things. Amen.

## Plea for Divine Help

HEAR us, Lord, holy Father, almighty and eternal God; and graciously send Your holy angel from heaven to watch over, to cherish, to protect, to abide with, and to defend all who dwell in this house. Through Christ our Lord. Amen.

## Prayer to Jesus

JESUS Christ, my God, I adore You and I thank You for the many favors You have bestowed on me this day. I offer You my sleep and all the moments of this night, and I pray You to preserve me from sin. Therefore, I place myself in Your most sacred Side, and under the mantle of our Blessed Lady, my Mother. May the holy angels assist me and keep me in peace, and may Your blessing be upon me.

## Prayer for the Home

WE BESEECH You, O Lord, to visit this home, and to drive far from it all the snares of the enemy: let Your holy angels dwell there so as to preserve us in peace; and let your blessing be always upon us. Through Christ our Lord. Amen.

## Prayer to the Guardian Angel

ANGEL of God, my guardian dear, to whom His love entrusts me here, ever this night be at my side, to light and guard, to rule and guide. Amen.

## Invocation to Jesus, Mary, and Joseph

JESUS, Mary, Joseph, I give You my heart and my soul.

Jesus, Mary, Joseph, assist me in my last agony. Jesus, Mary, Joseph, may I sleep and rest in peace with You.

# –5–

# Prayers to the Blessed Virgin Mary

## Prayer to Mary

O JESUS living in Mary, come and live in your servants, in the spirit of your holiness, in the fullness of your power, in the perfection of your ways, in the truth of your mysteries. Reign in us over all adverse powers by your Holy Spirit, and for the glory of the Father. Amen.

## We Fly to Your Patronage

WE FLY to your patronage, O holy Mother of God; despise not our petitions in our necessities, but deliver us always from all dangers, O glorious and blessed Virgin.

## Mary, Mother of Grace

MARY, Mother of grace, Mother of mercy, shield me from the enemy and receive me at the hour of my death.

## Holy Mary, Help the Helpless

HOLY Mary, help the helpless, strengthen the fearful, comfort the sorrowful, pray for the people, plead for the clergy, intercede for all women consecrated to God; may all who keep your sacred commemoration experience the might of your assistance.

*Partial indulgence.*

## Memorare

REMEMBER, O most gracious Virgin Mary, that never was it known that anyone who fled to your protection, implored your help or sought your intercession was left unaided. Inspired with this confidence, I fly to you, O Virgin of virgins, my Mother; to you do I come, before you I stand, sinful and sorrowful. O Mother of the Word Incarnate, despise not my petitions, but in your mercy hear and answer me. Amen.

*Partial indulgence.*

## Prayer to Our Lady of Fatima

O MOST holy Virgin Mary, Queen of the most holy Rosary, you were pleased to appear to the children of Fatima and reveal a glorious message. We implore you, inspire in our hearts a fervent love for the recitation of the Rosary. By meditating on the mysteries of the redemption that are recalled therein may we obtain the graces and virtues that we ask, through the merits of Jesus Christ, our Lord and Redeemer.

*Partial indulgence.*

## Prayer to Our Lady of Good Counsel

MOST glorious Virgin, you were chosen by the eternal Counsel to be the Mother of the eternal Word made flesh. You are the treasurer of divine graces and the advocate of sinners. I who am your most unworthy servant have recourse to you. Graciously be my guide and counselor in this valley of tears.

Obtain for me, through the Precious Blood of your divine Son, the forgiveness of my sins, the salvation of my soul, and the means necessary to obtain it. In like manner, obtain for holy Church victory over her enemies and the spread of Jesus' kingdom over the whole earth.

## Prayer to Our Lady of Guadalupe

OUR Lady of Guadalupe, mystical rose, intercede for the Church, protect the Holy Father, help all who invoke you in their necessities. Since you are the ever Virgin Mary and Mother of the true God, obtain for us from your most holy Son the grace of a firm and a sure hope amid the bitterness of life, as well as an ardent love and the precious gift of final perseverance.

## Our Lady, Help of Christians

MARY, powerful Virgin, you are the mighty and glorious protector of the Church. You are the marvelous help of Christians. You are awe-inspiring as an army in battle array. In the midst of our anguish, struggle, and distress, defend us from the power of the enemy, and at the hour of our death receive our soul in heaven.

## Our Lady of Lourdes

O IMMACULATE Virgin Mary, you are the refuge of sinners, the health of the sick, and the comfort of the afflicted. By your appearances at the Grotto of Lourdes you made it a privileged sanctuary where your favors are given to people streaming to it from the whole world. Over the years countless sufferers have obtained the cure of their infirmities—whether of soul, mind, or body. Therefore I come with limitless confidence to implore your motherly intercession.

# Prayers to the Blessed Virgin Mary for Every Day of the Week

## Sunday — Our Lady of the Trinity

OUR Lady of the Trinity,
Sunday is the Day of the Lord:
Father, Son, and Holy Spirit.
You are the beloved Daughter of the Father,
devoted Mother of the Son,
and exalted Bride of the Holy Spirit.
Help me to keep Sundays holy
by participating in the Eucharist
and dedicating myself to the things of God.

Grant that all the thoughts of my mind,
all the words of my mouth,
all the affections of my heart,
and all the actions of my life
may always be conformed to the Will of God.
Give me a great faith
to discern God here below,
in appearance and in a dark manner.
Then take me at last
to contemplate the ineffable Lord face to face
and to possess Him forever in heavenly glory
in union with you.

## Monday — Our Lady of Grace

OUR Lady of Grace,
Monday is the day of the Holy Spirit,
the Sanctifier.

Your soul was made full of grace
by the power of the Holy Spirit,
the third Person of the Trinity,
the uncreated love between the Father and the Son.
Through you I beg the merciful Father
to send the Holy Spirit of grace,
that He may bestow on me His sevenfold gifts.
May He send me the gift of *wisdom*,
which is none other than your Son Jesus;
the gift of *understanding*,
which will enlighten me;
the gift of *counsel*,
which will give me the strength to vanquish
the enemies of my sanctification and salvation.
May He impart to me the gift of *knowledge*,
which will enable me to discern
the teaching of your Son Jesus
and distinguish good from evil;
the gift of *piety*,
which will make me enjoy true peace;
and the gift of *fear of the Lord*,
which will make me shun all iniquity
and avoid all danger of offending
your Divine Son.

Pray for me,
O Lady of the Holy Spirit,
that I may be fruitful in good works
for the glory of God
and the spiritual and material good of all people.

## Tuesday — Queen of the Angels and Saints

QUEEN of the Angels and Saints,
Tuesday is the day of the Angels.
Help me to realize that in praising the Angels
I praise God's glory,
for by honoring them
I honor their Creator,
Who saw fit to send His Angels
to watch over His servants on earth.
Grant that I may be always under their protection
and one day enjoy their company in heaven.

Tuesday is also devoted to the Saints.
Enable me to see that God is glorified in them,
for their glory is the crowning of His gifts.
By their lives on earth,
He provides me with an example.
By my communion with them,
He gives me their friendship.
By their prayers,
He grants me strength and protection.
By this great company of witnesses,
He spurs me on to victory over evil
and the prize of eternal life.
Dear Mother Mary,
make me share the faith of the Saints on earth,
so that I may also experience their peace in heaven
together with you and your Divine Son.

## Wednesday — Spouse of Saint Joseph

SPOUSE of St. Joseph,
Wednesday is devoted to your husband,

the saintly carpenter who cared for you and Jesus
as part of the Holy Family.

In honor of this just man
who protected you and Jesus
from Herod who wanted to kill the Child,
save me from my many sins.
In honor of this foster father of Christ,
the Divine Physician,
sustain the sick and obtain relief for them.
In honor of this gentle man
who died in the arms of you and Jesus,
intercede for the dying.
In honor of this intrepid guardian
of the Holy Family,
protect all Christian families.
In honor of this dedicated and honest workman,
teach me to labor for Jesus.
In honor of this faithful and chaste spouse,
preserve in my heart
a love of fidelity and purity.
Dear Mother Mary,
let me always revere St. Joseph
and imitate his life of total dedication
to you and Jesus.

## Thursday — Our Lady of the Blessed Sacrament

OUR Lady of the Blessed Sacrament,
Thursday is devoted to the Blessed Sacrament
in commemoration of the Last Supper
when Jesus left us the Holy Sacrifice of the Mass,
the memorial of His Passion, Death, and Resurrection.

My Mother Mary,
thank you for having given me the Eucharistic Christ
Who offers Himself to the Father
as the Victim of Calvary at every Mass,
Who gives Himself to me
as food in Holy Communion,
and Who abides with me in the tabernacle
as the best Friend I have in the world.
For this reason I honor you
as Our Lady of the Blessed Sacrament.
Make me a frequent apostle of the Eucharist
and so Eucharist-minded
that my very life may be the Eucharist.

## Friday — Our Lady of Sorrows

OUR Lady of Sorrows,
during your life on earth,
you were saddened many times
and specifically during the traditional Seven Sorrows:
the prophecy of Simeon at the presentation,
the flight into Egypt,
the three days' loss of Jesus,
the meeting with Jesus carrying His Cross,
His Death on Calvary,
His being taken down from the Cross,
and His burial in the tomb.
Your sorrow on Calvary was deeper
than any sorrow felt on earth,
for no mother in all the world
had a heart as tender as your Heart,
which was the Heart of the Mother of God.
You bore your sufferings for us
that we might enjoy the graces of Redemption.

Dear Mother Mary,
console me when I am sad,
and make me happy with your Motherly love.
Comfort me when I am in pain,
and heal the wounds of my spirit.
Fill my heart with your joy,
and make me forget the troubles of this life,
so that I may be happy forever
with you and your Divine Son in heaven.

## Saturday — Our Lady, Queen of the World

HAIL, O Mother, Queen of the world.
You are the Mother of Fair Love,
you are the Mother of Jesus,
and the source of all grace,
the fragrance of all virtue,
the mirror of all purity.
You are joy in weeping,
victory in the struggle,
and hope in death.
How sweet is your name in my mouth,
what delightful harmony in my ears,
what intoxication in my heart!
You are the happiness of the suffering,
the crown of martyrs,
and the beauty of virgins.
Queen of glory and honor,
keep my soul from all danger.
Take my humble prayers
and bring them to God's throne in heaven
that they may be answered.
May I honor you
on earth with all human beings
and in heaven with all the Saints and Angels.

## Litany of the Blessed Virgin Mary

LORD, have mercy.
*Christ, have mercy.*
Lord, have mercy.
Christ, hear us.
*Christ, graciously hear us.*
God, the Father of heaven, *have mercy on us.*
God the Son, Redeemer of the world,
*have mercy on us.*
God the Holy Spirit,*
Holy Trinity, one God,*
Holy Mary, pray for us.**
Holy Mother of God,
Holy Virgin of virgins,
Mother of Christ,
Mother of the Church,
Mother of mercy,
Mother of divine grace,
Mother of hope,
Mother most pure,
Mother most chaste,
Mother inviolate,
Mother undefiled,
Mother most amiable,
Mother most admirable,
Mother of good counsel,
Mother of our Creator,
Mother of our Savior,
Virgin most prudent,
Virgin most venerable,
Virgin most renowned,
Virgin most powerful,

* *Have mercy on us* is repeated here.
** *Pray for us* is repeated after each invocation.

Virgin most merciful,
Virgin most faithful,
Mirror of justice,
Seat of wisdom,
Cause of our joy,
Spiritual vessel,
Vessel of honor,
Singular vessel of devotion,
Mystical rose,
Tower of David,
Tower of ivory,
House of gold,
Ark of the covenant,
Gate of heaven,
Morning star,
Health of the sick,
Refuge of sinners,
Solace of migrants,
Comforter of the afflicted,
Help of Christians,
Queen of angels,
Queen of patriarchs,
Queen of prophets,
Queen of apostles,
Queen of martyrs,
Queen of confessors,
Queen of virgins,
Queen of all saints,
Queen conceived without original sin,
Queen assumed into heaven,
Queen of the most holy Rosary,
Queen of families,
Queen of peace,

Lamb of God, You take away the sins of the world; *spare us, O Lord!*

Lamb of God, You take away the sins of the world; *graciously hear us, O Lord!*

Lamb of God, You take away the sins of the world; *have mercy on us.*

℣. Pray for us, O holy Mother of God.

℟. *That we may be made worthy of the promises of Christ.*

—6—

## Holy Mass

AT THE Last Supper, on the night when He was betrayed, our Savior instituted the Eucharistic sacrifice of His Body and Blood. He did this in order to perpetuate the sacrifice of the Cross throughout the centuries until He should come again, and so to entrust to His beloved Spouse, the Church, a memorial of His Death and Resurrection: a sacrament of love, a sign of unity, a bond of charity, a Paschal banquet in which Christ is eaten, the mind is filled with grace, and a pledge of future glory is given to us" (Vatican II: *Sacred Liturgy*, no. 47).

Thus the Mass is:

1) *the true sacrifice of the New Covenant*, in which a holy and living Victim is offered, Jesus Christ, and we in union with Him, as a gift of love and obedience to the Father;

2) a *sacred meal* and *spiritual banquet* of the children of God;

3) a *Paschal meal*, which evokes the passage (passover) of Jesus from this world to the Father; it renders Him present and makes Him live again in souls, and it anticipates our definitive passage to the Kingdom of God;

4) a *communitarian meal*, that is, a gathering together of the Head and His members, of Jesus and His Church, His Mystical Body, in order to carry out a perfect divine worship.

Thus, the Mass is the greatest prayer we have. Through it we give thanks and praise to the Father for the wonderful future He has given us in His Son. We also ask forgiveness for our sins and beg the Father's blessing upon ourselves and our fellow human beings.

# The Order of Mass

## THE INTRODUCTORY RITES

**Acts of prayer and penitence prepare us to meet Christ as he comes in Word and Sacrament. We gather in worship to celebrate our unity with him and with one another in faith.** ***STAND***

**Mass begins with an entrance procession of the ministers to the sanctuary, during which a chant is sung or the Entrance Antiphon of the day is recited.**

### GREETING (3 forms)

*Priest*: In the name of the Father, and of the Son, and of the Holy Spirit.

*People*: **Amen.**

**(a)**

*Priest*: The grace of our Lord Jesus Christ,
and the love of God,
and the communion of the Holy Spirit
be with you all.
*People*: **And with your spirit.**

**(b)**

*Priest*: Grace to you and peace from God our Father
and the Lord Jesus Christ.
*People*: **And with your spirit.**

**(c)**

*Priest*: The Lord be with you.
*People*: **And with your spirit.**

## THE PENITENTIAL ACT (3 forms)

*Priest*: Brethren (brothers and sisters), let us acknowledge our sins, and so prepare ourselves to celebrate the sacred mysteries.

**(a)**

*Priest* and *People*:

**I confess to almighty God
and to you, my brothers and sisters,
that I have greatly sinned,
in my thoughts and in my words,
in what I have done and in what I have failed to do,**
*And, striking their breast, they say:*
**through my fault, through my fault,
through my most grievous fault;**
*Then they continue:*
**therefore I ask blessed Mary ever-Virgin,
all the Angels and Saints,**

**and you, my brothers and sisters,**
**to pray for me to the Lord our God.**

**(b)**
*Priest*: Have mercy on us, O Lord.
*People*: **For we have sinned against you.**
*Priest*: Show us, O Lord, your mercy.
*People*: **And grant us your salvation.**

**(c)**
*Priest, or a Deacon or another minister*:
You were sent to heal the contrite of heart:
Lord, have mercy.
*People*: **Lord, have mercy.**
*Priest or other minister*:
You came to call sinners:
Christ, have mercy.
*People*: **Christ, have mercy.**
*Priest or other minister*:
You are seated at the right hand of the Father to intercede for us:
Lord, have mercy.
*People*: **Lord, have mercy.**

*At the end of any of the forms of the Penitential Act:*

*Priest*: May almighty God have mercy on us,
forgive us our sins, and bring us to everlasting life.
*People*: **Amen.**

## KYRIE

*Unless included in the Penitential Act, the Kyrie is sung or said by all, with alternating parts for the choir or cantor and for the people.*

℣. Lord, have mercy.
℟. **Lord, have mercy.**

℣. Christ, have mercy.
℟. **Christ, have mercy.**

℣. Lord, have mercy.
℟. **Lord, have mercy.**

## GLORIA

**As the Church assembled in the Spirit, we praise and pray to the Father and the Lamb.**

**Glory to God in the highest,
and on earth peace to people of good will.**

**We praise you,
we bless you,
we adore you,
we glorify you,
we give you thanks for your great glory,
Lord God, heavenly King,
O God, almighty Father.**

**Lord Jesus Christ, Only Begotten Son,
Lord God, Lamb of God, Son of the Father,
you take away the sins of the world,
have mercy on us;
you take away the sins of the world,
receive our prayer;
you are seated at the right hand of the Father,
have mercy on us.**

**For you alone are the Holy One,
you alone are the Lord,
you alone are the Most High,
Jesus Christ,
with the Holy Spirit,
in the glory of God the Father.
Amen.**

## COLLECT

*Priest*: Let us pray.

*Priest and people pray silently for a while. Then the Priest says the Collect prayer, at the end of which the people acclaim:*

*People*: **Amen.**

## THE LITURGY OF THE WORD

**The proclamation of God's Word is always centered on Christ, present through his Word. Old Testament writings prepare for him; New Testament books speak of him directly. All of scripture calls us to believe once more and to follow. After the reading we reflect upon God's words and respond to them.** *SIT*

### READINGS AND RESPONSORIAL PSALM

*At the end of the First Reading:*

*Reader*: The word of the Lord.

*People*: **Thanks be to God.**

*The people repeat the response sung by the cantor the first time and then after each verse.*

*At the end of the Second Reading:*

*Reader*: The word of the Lord.

*People*: **Thanks be to God.**

### GOSPEL ACCLAMATION (Alleluia)

*STAND*

*The people repeat the Alleluia after the cantor's Alleluia and then after the verse.*

*During Lent one of the following invocations is used as a response instead of the Alleluia:*

(1) **Glory and praise to you, Lord Jesus Christ!**

(2) **Glory to you, Lord Jesus Christ, Wisdom of God the Father!**

(3) **Glory to you, Word of God, Lord Jesus Christ!**

(4) **Glory to you, Lord Jesus Christ, Son of the living God!**

(5) **Praise and honor to you, Lord Jesus Christ!**

(6) **Praise to you, Lord Jesus Christ, King of endless glory!**

(7) **Marvelous and great are your works, O Lord!**

(8) **Salvation, glory, and power to the Lord Jesus Christ!**

## GOSPEL

*Deacon (or Priest)*: The Lord be with you.
*People*: **And with your spirit.**
*Deacon (or Priest)*:
✠ A reading from the holy Gospel according to *N.*
*People*: **Glory to you, O Lord.**

*At the end*:
*Deacon (or Priest)*: The Gospel of the Lord.
*People*: **Praise to you, Lord Jesus Christ.** *SIT*

## HOMILY

**God's Word is spoken again in the Homily. The Holy Spirit speaking through the lips of the preacher explains and applies today's biblical readings to the needs of this particular congregation. He calls us to respond to Christ through the life we lead.**

## PROFESSION OF FAITH (Creed)

As a people we express our acceptance of God's message in the Scriptures and the Homily. We summarize our faith by proclaiming a creed handed down from the early Church.

*All say the Profession of Faith on Sundays.*

### The Nicene Creed

*STAND*

I believe in one God,
the Father almighty,
maker of heaven and earth,
of all things visible and invisible.

I believe in one Lord Jesus Christ,
the Only Begotten Son of God,
born of the Father before all ages.
God from God, Light from Light,
true God from true God,
begotten, not made, consubstantial with the Father;
through him all things were made.
For us men and for our salvation
he came down from heaven,

*At the words that follow, up to and including and became man, all bow.*

and by the Holy Spirit was incarnate of the Virgin Mary, and became man.

For our sake he was crucified under Pontius Pilate,
he suffered death and was buried,

and rose again on the third day
in accordance with the Scriptures.
He ascended into heaven
and is seated at the right hand of the Father.
He will come again in glory
to judge the living and the dead
and his kingdom will have no end.

I believe in the Holy Spirit, the Lord, the giver of life,
who proceeds from the Father and the Son,
who with the Father and the Son is adored and glorified,
who has spoken through the prophets.

I believe in one, holy, catholic and apostolic Church.
I confess one Baptism for the forgiveness of sins
and I look forward to the resurrection of the dead
and the life of the world to come. Amen.

*OR*

### The Apostles' Creed

I believe in God,
the Father almighty,
Creator of heaven and earth,
and in Jesus Christ, his only Son, our Lord,

*At the words that follow, up to and including the Virgin Mary, all bow.*

who was conceived by the Holy Spirit,
born of the Virgin Mary,
suffered under Pontius Pilate,
was crucified, died and was buried;
he descended into hell;

on the third day he rose again from the dead;
he ascended into heaven,
and is seated at the right hand of God the Father almighty;
from there he will come to judge the living and the dead.

I believe in the Holy Spirit,
the holy catholic Church,
the communion of saints,
the forgiveness of sins,
the resurrection of the body,
and life everlasting. Amen.

### UNIVERSAL PRAYER (Prayer of the Faithful)

**As a priestly people we unite with one another to pray for today's needs in the Church and the world.**

*After the Priest's introduction the Deacon or other minister sings or says the invocations.*

*People*: Lord, hear our prayer.
*(or other response, according to local custom)*

*At the end the Priest says the concluding prayer:*

*People*: Amen.

## THE LITURGY OF THE EUCHARIST

**Made ready by reflection on God's Word, we enter now into the eucharistic sacrifice itself, the Supper of the Lord. We celebrate the memorial which the Lord instituted at his Last Supper. We are God's new people, the redeemed brothers and sisters of Christ, gathered by him around his table. We are here to bless God and to receive the gift of Jesus' Body and Blood so that our faith and life may be transformed.**

## PREPARATION OF THE GIFTS

*SIT*

**The bread and wine for the Eucharist, with our gifts for the Church and the poor, are gathered and brought to the altar. We prepare our hearts by song or in silence as the Lord's table is being set.**

*Priest*:

Blessed are you, Lord God of all creation,
for through your goodness we have received
the bread we offer you:
fruit of the earth and work of human hands,
it will become for us the bread of life.

*If there is no singing, the Priest may say this prayer aloud, and the people may respond*:

*People*: **Blessed be God for ever.**

*Priest*:

By the mystery of this water and wine
may we come to share in the divinity of Christ
who humbled himself to share in our humanity.

Blessed are you, Lord God of all creation,
for through your goodness we have received
the wine we offer you:
fruit of the vine and work of human hands,
it will become our spiritual drink.

*If there is no singing, the Priest may say this prayer aloud, and the people may respond:*

*People*: **Blessed be God for ever.**

## INVITATION TO PRAYER

*Priest*: Pray, brethren (brothers and sisters),
that my sacrifice and yours
may be acceptable to God,
the almighty Father. ***STAND***

*People*: **May the Lord accept the sacrifice at your hands**
**for the praise and glory of his name,**
**for our good**
**and the good of all his holy Church.**

*The Priest, speaking in our name, says the Prayer over the Offerings, asking the Father to bless and accept these gifts.*

*People*: **Amen.**

## EUCHARISTIC PRAYER

**We begin the eucharistic service of praise and thanksgiving, the center of the entire celebration, the central prayer of worship. We lift our hearts to God, and offer praise and thanks as the Priest addresses this prayer to the Father through Jesus Christ. Together we join Christ in his sacrifice, celebrating his memorial in the holy meal and acknowledging with him the wonderful works of God in our lives.**

## PREFACE DIALOGUE

*Priest*: The Lord be with you.
*People*: **And with your spirit.**
*Priest*: Lift up your hearts.
*People*: **We lift them up to the Lord.**
*Priest*: Let us give thanks to the Lord our God.
*People*: **It is right and just.**

*The Priest says the Preface here.*

## PREFACE ACCLAMATION (Holy, Holy, Holy)

*Priest and People*:

**Holy, Holy, Holy Lord God of hosts.
Heaven and earth are full of your glory.
Hosanna in the highest.
Blessed is he who comes in the name of the Lord.
Hosanna in the highest.** *KNEEL*

### Memorial Acclamation

*Priest*: The mystery of faith.
*People*:

(a) **We proclaim your Death, O Lord,
and profess your Resurrection
until you come again.**

(b) **When we eat this Bread and drink this Cup,
we proclaim your Death, O Lord,
until you come again.**

(c) **Save us, Savior of the world,
for by your Cross and Resurrection
you have set us free.**

### Great Amen

*Priest*: . . . for ever and ever.
*People*: **Amen.**

## THE COMMUNION RITE

**To prepare for the paschal meal, to welcome the Lord, we pray for forgiveness and exchange a sign of peace. Before eating Christ's Body and drinking his Blood, we must be one with him.** *STAND*

## THE LORD'S PRAYER

**The Priest asks the people to join him in the prayer that Jesus taught us.**

*Priest and People:*

**Our Father, who art in heaven,**
**hallowed be thy name;**
**thy kingdom come,**
**thy will be done**
**on earth as it is in heaven.**
**Give us this day our daily bread,**
**and forgive us our trespasses,**
**as we forgive those who trespass against us;**
**and lead us not into temptation,**
**but deliver us from evil.**

*Priest*: Deliver us, Lord, we pray, from every evil,
graciously grant peace in our days,
that, by the help of your mercy,
we may be always free from sin
and safe from all distress,
as we await the blessed hope
and the coming of our Savior, Jesus Christ.

*People*: **For the kingdom,**
**the power and the glory are yours**
**now and for ever.**

## SIGN OF PEACE

*The Priest says the prayer for peace*:

Lord Jesus Christ,
who said to your Apostles:
Peace I leave you, my peace I give you,
look not on our sins,
but on the faith of your Church,

and graciously grant her peace and unity
in accordance with your will.
Who live and reign for ever and ever.
*People*: **Amen.**
*Priest*: The peace of the Lord be with you always.
*People*: **And with your spirit.**
*Deacon* (or *Priest*):
Let us offer each other the sign of peace.
*The people exchange a sign of peace and charity, according to local custom.*

## LAMB OF GOD

*The Priest breaks the host over the paten and places a small piece in the chalice, saying quietly:*
May this mingling of the Body and Blood
of our Lord Jesus Christ
bring eternal life to us who receive it.

*Meanwhile the following is sung or said:*
**Lamb of God, you take away**
**the sins of the world, have mercy on us.**
**Lamb of God, you take away**
**the sins of the world, have mercy on us.**
**Lamb of God, you take away**
**the sins of the world, grant us peace.**

*The invocation may even be repeated several times if the breaking of the bread is prolonged. Only the final time, however, is grant us peace said.*

*KNEEL*

*The Priest prays quietly before Communion.*

## INVITATION TO COMMUNION

*The Priest genuflects, takes the host and, holding it slightly raised above the paten or above the chalice, while facing the people, says aloud:*

*Priest*: Behold the Lamb of God,
behold him who takes away the sins of the world.
Blessed are those called to the supper of the Lamb.
*Priest and People (once only)*:
**Lord, I am not worthy**
**that you should enter under my roof,**
**but only say the word**
**and my soul shall be healed.**
*Priest*: The Body of Christ.
*Communicant*: **Amen.**
*Priest*: The Blood of Christ.
*Communicant*: **Amen.**

*The Communion Chant or other appropriate song or hymn is sung while Communion is given to the faithful. If there is no singing, the Communion Antiphon is said.* ***STAND***

## PRAYER AFTER COMMUNION

**The Priest prays in our name that we may live the life of faith since we have been strengthened by Christ himself. Our *Amen* makes his prayer our own.**

*Priest*: Let us pray.
*At the end, People*: Amen.

## THE CONCLUDING RITES

**We have heard God's Word and eaten the Body of Christ. Now it is time for us to leave, to do good works, to praise and bless the Lord in our daily lives.** ***STAND***

### SOLEMN BLESSING

*Priest*: The Lord be with you.
*People*: ***And with your spirit.***

### FINAL BLESSING

*Priest*: May almighty God bless you,
the Father, and the Son, ✠ and the Holy Spirit.
*People*: **Amen.**

### DISMISSAL

*Deacon* (or *Priest*):
(a) Go forth, the Mass is ended.
(b) Go and announce the Gospel of the Lord.
(c) Go in peace, glorifying the Lord by your life.
(d) Go in peace.

*People*: **Thanks be to God.**

## –7–

## Prayers for Confession

**THIS Sacrament now contains a more communitarian dimension, showing that it is part of the Church's work of reconciling sinners to God. It also contains elements of thanksgiving and praise to God for salvation. Finally, it shines out with the paschal joy of those who have been redeemed by the Son of God.**

**When we go to confession, we should:**

1. **Ask ourselves how we have offended God.**
2. **Be truly sorry for our sins.**
3. **Make up our minds not to sin again.**
4. **Tell our sins to the Priest.**
5. **Do the penance the Priest gives us.**

## Prayer before Confession

MY LORD and God, I have sinned. I am guilty before You.

Grant me the strength to say to Your minister what I say to You in the secret of my heart.

Increase my repentance. Make it more genuine. May it be really a sorrow for having offended You and my neighbor rather than a wounded love of self.

Help me to atone for my sin. May the sufferings of my life and my little mortifications be joined with the sufferings of Jesus, Your Son, and cooperate in rooting sin from the world.

## Examination of Conscience

- How long has it been since my last confession?
- Did I conceal any sin?
- Did I say my penance?
- Have I neglected my home and my family duties, or my work?
- Have I been lazy, neglectful, or willfully distracted during prayer or at Mass?
- Have I used God's name irreverently, or taken false or needless oaths?
- Have I missed Mass through my own fault on Sundays or holydays, or worked unnecessarily on Sunday?
- Have I disobeyed, angered, or been disrespectful toward my parents, teachers, employers, or other superiors?
- Have I been unjust and unkind to those over whom I have authority?
- Have I quarreled with or willfully hurt anyone?
- Have I been guilty of cruelty, mental or physical, toward anyone?

- Have I caused another to commit sin?
- Have I offended in any way by thought, word, or deed against purity?
- Have I led others into sin?
- Have I stolen or destroyed property belonging to any other person or company?
- Have I given a bad example to the members of my family or others?
- Have I knowingly accepted stolen goods?
- Have I paid all my just debts?
- Have I told lies, repeated harmful gossip, or injured another person's character?
- Have I been sinfully angry, greedy, proud, envious, jealous, or intemperate in eating or drinking?
- Have I willfully broken any of the Church laws concerning fast or abstinence?
- Have I failed to support my Church?
- Have I received Communion during Easter Time?

*For married people:*

- Have I failed to show love, respect, and good example toward my partner?
- Have I neglected my duty to my children in regard to their religious instruction, to their training in good habits, and to their schooling?
- Have I sinned against the duties of married life?

We must confess the number of our sins as best we can remember them.

## CELEBRATION OF THE SACRAMENT OF PENANCE

### 1. The Reception of the Penitent

When the penitent comes to confess his (her) sins, the Priest welcomes him (her) with kindness and greets him (her) with friendly words.

*Penitent*:

**In the name of the Father, and of the Son, and of the Holy Spirit. Amen.**

*Priest*:

May God who has shone his light in our hearts
grant that you may truly know your sins
and his mercy.

*Penitent*: **Amen.**

## 2. The Reading of the Word of God

**The Priest may read a text of Sacred Scripture that announces God's mercy and calls people to conversion.**

## 3. The Confession of Sins and the Acceptance of Satisfaction

**The penitent tells the Priest when he (she) last celebrated the Sacrament and then confesses his (her) sins, asking appropriate questions, if necessary. The penitent then listens to any advice the Priest may give and accepts the satisfaction (or "penance") from the Priest.**

## 4. The Prayer of the Penitent and the Absolution

**The Priest then invites the penitent to express his (her) contrition, which the penitent may do in these or similar words:**

**O my God,**
**I am sorry and repent with all my heart**
**for all the wrong I have done**
**and for the good I have failed to do,**
**because by sinning I have offended you,**
**who are all good and worthy to be loved above all things.**
**I firmly resolve, with the help of your grace,**

**to do penance,**
**to sin no more,**
**and to avoid the occasions of sin.**
**Through the merits of the Passion of our Savior Jesus Christ,**
**Lord, have mercy.**

**Other options may be used.**

**The Priest extends his hands (or at least extends his right hand) and says:**

God, the Father of mercies,
through the Death and Resurrection of his Son
has reconciled the world to himself
and poured out the Holy Spirit for the forgiveness of sins;
through the ministry of the Church
may God grant you pardon and peace.
AND I ABSOLVE YOU FROM YOUR SINS,
IN THE NAME OF THE FATHER, AND OF THE SON, ✠ AND OF THE HOLY SPIRIT.

## 5. The Proclamation of Praise of God and the Dismissal of the Penitent

**After the absolution:**

*Priest*:
Give thanks to the Lord, for he is good.

*Penitent*:
**For his mercy endures for ever.**

**Then the Priest dismisses the penitent:**

*Priest*:
The Lord has forgiven your sins.
Go in peace.

**The Priest may use these or other words of dismissal.**

*–8–*

# Prayers before Holy Communion
## (1st Series)

### Prayer of St. Ambrose

LORD Jesus Christ,
I approach Your banquet table
in fear and trembling,
for I am a sinner,
and dare not rely on my own worth
but only on Your goodness and mercy.
I am defiled by many sins in body and soul,
and by my unguarded thoughts and words.

Gracious God of majesty and awe,
I seek Your protection,
I look for Your healing.
Poor troubled sinner that I am,
I appeal to You, the fountain of all mercy.
I cannot bear Your judgment,
but I trust in Your salvation.

Lord, I show my wounds to You
and uncover my shame before You.
I know my sins are many and great,
and they fill me with fear,
but I hope in Your mercies,
for they cannot be numbered.

Lord Jesus Christ, eternal King, God and Man,
crucified for humankind,
look upon me with mercy and hear my prayer,
for I trust in You.
Have mercy on me,

full of sorrow and sin,
for the depth of Your compassion never ends.

Praise to You, saving sacrifice,
offered on the wood of the Cross for me and for all humankind.
Praise to the noble and precious Blood,
flowing from the wounds of my crucified Lord Jesus Christ
and washing away the sins of the whole world.
Remember, Lord, Your creature,
whom You have redeemed with Your Blood.
I repent my sins,
and I long to put right what I have done.
Merciful Father, take away all my offenses and sins;
purify me in body and soul,
and make me worthy to taste the Holy of Holies.

May Your Body and Blood,
which I intend to receive, although I am unworthy,
be for me the remission of my sins,
the washing away of my guilt,
the end of my evil thoughts,
and the rebirth of my better instincts.

May it inspire me to do the works pleasing to You
and profitable to my health in body and soul,
and be a firm defense against the wiles of my enemies.

## Prayer of St. Thomas Aquinas

ALMIGHTY and ever-living God,
I approach the Sacrament of Your only-begotten Son,
our Lord Jesus Christ.

I come sick to the doctor of life,
unclean to the fountain of mercy,
blind to the radiance of eternal light,
and poor and needy to the Lord of heaven and earth.
Lord, in Your great generosity,
heal my sickness, wash away my defilement,
enlighten my blindness, enrich my poverty,
and clothe my nakedness.

May I receive the Bread of Angels,
the King of kings and Lord of lords,
with humble reverence,
with the purity and faith,
the repentance and love, and the determined purpose
that will help to bring me to salvation.
May I receive the Sacrament
of the Lord's Body and Blood,
and its reality and power.

Kind God,
may I receive the Body of Your only-begotten Son,
our Lord Jesus Christ,
born from the womb of the Virgin Mary,
and so be received into His Mystical Body
and numbered among His members.
Loving Father,
as on my earthly pilgrimage
I now receive Your beloved Son
under the veil of a Sacrament,
may I one day see Him face to face in glory,
Who lives and reigns with You for ever.

# Prayers before Holy Communion
## (2nd Series)

### Act of Faith

LORD Jesus Christ,
I firmly believe that You are present
in this Blessed Sacrament
as true God and true Man,
with Your Body and Blood,
Soul and Divinity.
My Redeemer and my Judge,
I adore Your Divine Majesty
in union with the Angels and Saints.
I believe, O Lord;
increase my faith.

### Act of Hope

GOOD Jesus,
in You alone I place all my hope.
You are my salvation and my strength,
the source of all good.
Through Your mercy,
through Your Passion and Death,
I hope to obtain the pardon of my sins,
the grace of final perseverance,
and a happy eternity.

### Act of Love

JESUS, my God,
I love You with my whole heart
and above all things,
because You are the one supreme Good
and an infinitely perfect Being.

You have given Your life for me, a poor sinner,
and in Your mercy
You have even offered Yourself
as Food for my soul.

My God,
I love You.
Inflame my heart
so that I may love You more.

## Act of Contrition

O MY Savior,
I am truly sorry for having offended You
because You are infinitely good
and sin displeases You.
I detest all the sins of my life
and I desire to atone for them.
Through the merits of Your Precious Blood,
wash me of all stain of sin,
so that entirely cleansed
I may worthily approach
the most holy Sacrament of the altar.

## Act of Desire

JESUS,
my God and my all,
my soul longs for You.
My heart yearns to receive You
in Holy Communion.
Come, Bread of Heaven and Food of Angels,
to nourish my soul
and rejoice my heart.
Come, most lovable Friend of my soul,
to inflame me with such love
that I may never again be separated from You.

# Prayers before Holy Communion
## (3rd Series)

### Act of Faith

O JESUS,
my light and sanctification,
open the eyes of my mind,
and fill my soul with Your grace
that I may know the importance of the action
that I am about to perform.
Let me consider how sacred and exalted
is He Whom I am about to receive.
I am about to receive within my heart and soul
my God, my Creator, my Savior,
my sovereign Lord, my Jesus.

I am about to receive within my breast
really and truly
that same Jesus
Who is the life, glory, treasure,
the love and delight of the eternal Father;
that same Jesus
Whom so many Patriarchs, Prophets, and Just of the Old Testament
desired to see and did not see;
that same Jesus
Who lived and walked on earth,
eating and drinking in the company of sinners;
that same Jesus
Who was nailed to the Cross,
Whose Body was bruised, wounded, and immolated for me and all human beings.

I am about to receive that same Savior
Who ascended gloriously into heaven,
Who sits at the right hand of the Father,
and Who will come again at the end of time,
clothed in power and majesty,
to judge the world.
O my God,
how unworthy I am of such a great favor.
I acknowledge this in the presence
of both heaven and earth.

*St. John Eudes (adapted)*

## Act of Contrition

O GOD,
loose, remit, and forgive my sins against You,
whether in word, in deed, or in thought;
and whether they are willingly or unwillingly,
knowingly or unknowingly committed,
forgive them all.
For You are good and You love all human beings.
And through the prayers of Your most holy Mother,
or Your heavenly servants and holy spirits,
and all the Saints who have found favor with You,
enable me to receive without condemnation
Your holy Body and Your Precious Blood.
Let my soul and body be thus healed
and my evil imaginings be driven away,
for Yours is the Kingdom, the power, and the glory:
Father, Son, and Holy Spirit,
now and forever.

*St. John Chrysostom (adapted)*

## Act of Petition

GIVE me Yourself,
O my God,
give Yourself to me.
Behold, I love You,
and if my love is too weak a thing,
grant me to love You more strongly.
I cannot measure my love to know
how much it falls short of being sufficient,
but let my soul hasten to Your embrace
and never be turned away
until it is hidden in the secret shelter
of Your presence.

This only do I know,
that it is not good for me
when You are not with me,
when You are only outside me.
I want You in my very self.
All the plenty in the world
that is not my God
is utter want.

*St. Augustine of Hippo*

# Prayers before Holy Communion (4th Series)

## Act of Faith

JESUS,
I believe that Holy Communion
gives me claim to all the actual graces
that I need to be holy
and to imitate You,
my Divine Master.

With Your grace I can live as a sincere Christian—
in some way as "another Christ"
among my fellow human beings.
Every act of virtue is derived from Your grace.

You are not only the model of all virtues
but also One Who merited for us
the grace to practice them.
You are the source of spiritual perfection.
Help me to foster a lively faith
in the mystery of grace
through which You will act in me,
because without Your grace I can do nothing.
Your grace will help me
to maintain the spirit of devotion
that should underlie my Christian life.

## Act of Preparation

LORD, I am preparing to meet You at Mass.
I am coming as I am,
no change of feelings or of thoughts,
just as I am living my life today, every day.
I am coming to meet You;
I know You are present in the Mass,
that You are the Christ
—born, dead, risen, ascended to the Father.

I am coming to measure my life in You,
to change myself;
You invite us to be "new,"
or we will not be Christians.

I am coming to bring You
what I am every day,
what I have every day;
in me are present at this moment

my dear ones, my friends,
all the people of the world;
the people I meet,
with whom I speak and work,
with whom I discuss and argue;
all my usual gestures,
all the things I use and deal with,
all the realities and situations
in which I am involved.

I am coming to be saved by You,
the Paschal Mystery,
because I, too, a "lay person,"
"co-celebrate" the Mass
whenever I am with You, Christ,
and strive to bring all back to the Father;
I work in You, with You, and for You,
my "passing"
from mine to Your life,
from Yours to my life,
from mine to Your love,
from Yours to my love:
every day, every instant.

Lord, I am coming to Mass to understand
and to renew my place in the world,
in my family,
in my job,
in the Church,
in my encounters with others.

Lord, I am coming to learn that this possibility
of love, life, salvation,
is a gift from You.
I am coming because I am not able
to love truly.

*Anna Teresa Ciccolini*

*—9—*

# Prayers after Holy Communion
## (1st Series)

### Prayer of St. Thomas Aquinas

LORD, Father all-powerful and ever-living God,
I thank You,
for even though I am a sinner,
Your unprofitable servant,
not because of my worth
but in the kindness of Your mercy,
You have fed me
with the precious Body and Blood of Your Son,
our Lord Jesus Christ.
I pray that this Holy Communion
may not bring me condemnation and punishment
but forgiveness and salvation.

May it be a helmet of faith
and a shield of goodwill.
May it purify me from evil ways
and put an end to my evil passions.
May it bring me charity and patience,
humility and obedience,
and growth in the power to do good.
May it be my strong defense
against all my enemies, visible and invisible,
and the perfect calming of all my evil impulses,
bodily and spiritual.
May it unite me more closely to You,
the one true God,
and lead me safely through death
to everlasting happiness with You.

And I pray that You will lead me, a sinner,
to the banquet where You,
with Your Son and Holy Spirit,
are true and perfect light,
total fulfillment, everlasting joy,
gladness without end,
and perfect happiness to Your Saints.
Grant this through Christ our Lord.

## Prayer to Our Redeemer

SOUL of Christ, make me holy.
Body of Christ, be my salvation.
Blood of Christ, let me drink Your wine.
Water flowing from the side of Christ, wash me clean.
Passion of Christ, strengthen me.
Kind Jesus, hear my prayer;
hide me within Your wounds
and keep me close to You.
Defend me from the evil enemy.
Call me at my death
to the fellowship of Your Saints,
that I may sing Your praise with them
through all eternity.

## Prayer of Self-Dedication to Jesus Christ

LORD Jesus Christ,
take all my freedom,
my memory, my understanding, and my will.
All that I have and cherish You have given me.
I surrender it all to be guided by Your Will.
Your grace and Your love are wealth enough for me.
Give me these, Lord Jesus, and I ask for nothing more.

# Prayers after Holy Communion
## (2nd Series)

### Act of Faith

JESUS,
I firmly believe that You are present within me
as God and Man,
to enrich my soul with graces and to fill my heart
with the happiness of the Blessed.
I believe that You are Christ, the Son of the living God.

### Act of Adoration

WITH deepest humility,
I adore You,
my Lord and my God;
You have made my soul Your dwelling place.
I adore You as my Creator
from Whose hands I came
and with Whom I am to be happy forever.

### Act of Love

DEAR Jesus,
I love You with my whole heart,
with my whole soul, and with all my strength.
May the love of Your own Sacred Heart
fill my soul and purify it
so that I may die to the world for love of You,
as You died on the Cross for love of me.
My God, You are all mine;
grant that I may be all Yours in time and in eternity.

### Act of Thanksgiving

DEAR Lord,
I thank You from the depths of my heart
for Your infinite kindness in coming to me.
With Your most holy Mother
and all the Angels,
I praise Your mercy and generosity
toward me, a poor sinner.
I thank You for nourishing my soul
with Your Sacred Body and Precious Blood.
I will try to show my gratitude to You
in the Sacrament of Your love,
by obedience to Your holy commandments,
by fidelity to my duties,
by kindness to my neighbor,
and by an earnest endeavor
to become more like You in my daily conduct.

## Prayers after Holy Communion
## (3rd Series)

### Act of Offering

O KIND Father,
I offer You this holy Sacrament
with all the merits and virtues of Your beloved Son
for me, Your poor creature,
with such love and fidelity
as Christ Himself offered it
for the salvation of the world.
I offer it for all the benefits
that You have showered on me

from my birth until this day.
You created me by Your goodness,
redeemed me by Your Son,
sanctified me by Your Holy Spirit,
endowed me with imperishable goods by Your grace,
and guarded me from many misfortunes
and countless sins.

As an adequate return for these favors,
I offer You all the praise and thanks
that Your beloved Son, Jesus, ever gave
while He yet lived on earth,
and that He still renders to You in heaven.
I offer You this holy Sacrament
in compensation for all the virtues
that I ought to possess, yet do not,
and for obtaining all the necessary graces
of which I stand in need for Your holy service.

I also offer it for the pardon of all the sins
that I have committed,
and in satisfaction for all the negligence and remissness into which I have fallen.
Because I have deserved so much and such heavy punishment
that I can never be in a position
to satisfy for everything,
I have recourse to the immeasurable treasure
of the merits of Your dear Son,
Whom I now bear in my heart.
I wish to pay my debt honorably and fully
by this means.

*Sts. Gertrude and Mechtilde*

## Act of Admiration

O JESUS,
my God, my Creator, my Savior, and my Lord,
what a wonderful thing it is for me
to possess You really at this moment!
The One Who dwells from all eternity
in the bosom of the Father
has come into my innermost being. . . .
Even the Divinity,
the most Holy Trinity,
all that is most admirable in God
and in all heaven has come down to me,
a poor and unworthy creature.

O God,
how good and merciful You are.
What can I say or what can I do
in the presence of things so great and marvelous?
Lord Jesus,
let all my faculties render homage and adoration
to You.
But, my God,
what temerity on my part
to have received You—You, the Holy of Holies—
into an abode so impure
and with so little love and preparation!
I ask Your forgiveness for this
and for all sins and ingratitude of my past life.

*St. John Eudes*

## Act of Hope

FOR Your mercies' sake,
O Lord, my God,
tell me what You are to me.

Say to my soul: "I am your salvation."
So speak that I may hear,
O Lord;
my heart is listening;
open it that it may hear You,
and say to my soul: "I am your salvation."
After hearing this word,
may I come in haste to take hold of You.
Hide not Your face from me.
Let me see Your face even if I die,
lest I die with longing to see it.

The house of my soul is too small to receive You;
let it be enlarged by You.
It is all in ruins;
do You repair it.
There are things in it—
I confess and I know—
that must offend Your sight.
But who shall cleanse it?
Or to what other besides You shall I cry out?
From my secret sins cleanse me, O Lord,
and from those of others spare Your servant.

*St. Augustine of Hippo*

## Prayer to Be a Victim of Love

DIVINE Word,
worthy of all admiration and all love,
You draw me continually to Yourself.
You came into this world of exile
ready to suffer and die,
so as to bring souls within their true orbit,
the bosom of the Blessed Trinity.
And now, reascended into the inaccessible light
that is evermore Your dwelling place,

You still frequent this valley of tears,
hidden under the appearance of the Sacred Host.
You are still ready to feed my soul
with Your own Divinity—
my poor soul that would sink back into nothingness at any moment
if You did not give it life with a simple glance!

O Jesus,
my gratitude bids me say that You love me fondly;
and when I meet with such fondness from You,
how can my heart fail to go out to You—
how can any heart fail to go out to You—
and how can my trust in You have any limits? . . .
One day, I hope, You will come down
to carry off this poor creature of Yours,
to carry it up to the very center of love,
and consume it in love's furnace,
to which it has offered itself as a victim.

*St. Thérèse of Lisieux*

## Act of Desire to Proclaim Christ

DEAR Jesus,
help me to spread Your fragrance everywhere I go.
Flood my soul with Your Spirit and Life.
Penetrate and possess my whole being so utterly
that my life may only be a radiance of Yours.
Shine through me and be so in me
that every soul I come in contact with
may feel Your presence in my soul.

Let them look up,
and see no longer me,
but only Jesus!
Stay with me

and then I will begin to shine as You shine,
so to shine as to be a light to others.

The light,
O Jesus,
will be all from You;
none of it will be mine.
It will be You, shining on others through me.
Let me thus praise You
in the way that You love best,
by shining on those around me.
Let me preach You without preaching,
not by words but by example,
by the catching force,
the sympathetic influence of what I do,
the evident fullness of the love
my heart bears for You.

*St. John Newman*

## Prayers after Holy Communion
## (4th Series)

### Prayer to Be Renewed

LORD, it makes no sense
to speak of Eucharist, Mass,
Communion, Encounter,
if I don't let myself
be "made new" by You.

To become truly
and continuously
new in love,
a love that I am not able to retain consistently,
but that I often replace with a surrogate,
or an educated selfishness.

Lord, I have met with You
in this Mass;
to become new means to discover
that this old man,
this coughing, clumsy bundle,
is my brother;
that this silly looking little woman
mumbling and fingering her rosary
is my sister;
really and truly.
I am going to move closer and smile
and exchange a word.

It means to open the door of the church
to start a new way of loving,
as lovers of God and human beings.
Exactly like "lovers."

*Anna Teresa Ciccolini*

## Prayer to See Jesus in Others

THROUGH this Holy Communion,
I beg You, O Lord Jesus,
for the grace ever to love You
in my neighbor.
Let me see in every human being
Your own dear Self—disguised but really there.
Since every human being is a potential member
of Your Mystical Body,
I want to make my every act
a personal service rendered to You.

Your new law demands that I avoid
not only bodily injury to my neighbor
but also angry and uncharitable words and emotions.

Let me never put limits to my forgiveness,
so that Your Father may forgive me my offenses.
Through this Communion
make me a living example
of Your great commandment of love.

## –10–

# Prayers before the Blessed Sacrament

### MEDITATION

The Eucharist is reserved in our churches to be a powerful help to prayer and the service of others. Reservation of the Blessed Sacrament means that at the end of Communion the remaining Consecrated Bread is placed in the tabernacle and reverently reserved. The Eucharist reserved is a continuing sign of our Lord's real presence among His people and spiritual food for the sick and dying.

We owe gratitude, adoration, and devotion to the Real Presence of Christ in the Blessed Sacrament reserved. We show this devotion in our visits to the tabernacle in our churches and in Benediction when the Blessed Sacrament is exposed to the people for reverence and adoration and the priest blesses the people with the Lord's Body.

The tombs of the Martyrs, the paintings on the walls in the catacombs, and the custom of reserving the Blessed Sacrament in the homes of the first Christians in the years of persecution show the unity of faith in the first centuries of Christianity in the doctrine that in the Eucharist Christ is really contained, offered, and received. From the Eucharist the entire Church drew strength for courageous struggles and brilliant victories.

The Eucharist is the center of all Sacramental life because it is of the greatest importance for uniting and strengthening the Church.

## Act of Desire

JESUS,
I come to You.
You are the Way that I want to follow
in obedience to Your commandments,
Your counsels, and Your example.
Let me walk after You
in the way of obedience, self-denial, and sacrifice
that leads to heaven and to You.

Jesus,
You are the Truth.
You are the true Light that enlightens
everyone who comes into the world.
I believe in You.
I believe in Your Gospel.
I want to know You that I may love You.
I want to make You known
in order to make You loved.

Jesus,
You are the Life,
through Your sanctifying grace
that is the life of our souls;
through Your words
that are "the words of everlasting life";
through Your Eucharist
that is "the living Bread that has come down from heaven";

through Your Heart that is the fountain of life
for individual souls and for society.

I cling to Your Word with all my heart.
I hunger for the living Bread of Your Eucharist.
I open my heart eagerly to the life-giving streams from Your Sacred Heart.
I unite myself inwardly to all Its intentions.
May this Divine Heart reign universally
over the children of the Church
and over all humanity. Amen.

## Prayer to Return Christ's Love

MY LOVING Jesus,
behold to what lengths
Your boundless love has gone!
From Your own Flesh and Precious Blood,
You have prepared for me a Divine Table
in order to give Yourself to me.

What has impelled You
to this excess of love?
Nothing else surely
except Your most loving Heart.

O adorable Heart of my Jesus,
burning furnace of Divine Love,
receive my heart
within Your most sacred Wound,
in order that,
in this school of love,
I may learn to make
a return of love
to the God Who has given me
such wondrous proofs of His great love. Amen.

## Prayer of Adoration and Petition

I ADORE You, O Jesus,
true God and true Man,
here present in the Holy Eucharist,
as I humbly kneel before You
and unite myself in spirit
with all the faithful on earth
and all the Saints in heaven.

In heartfelt gratitude for so great a blessing,
I love You, my Jesus,
with my whole soul,
for You are infinitely perfect
and all worthy of my love.
Give me the grace
nevermore in any way to offend You.

Grant that I may be renewed
by Your Eucharistic presence here on earth
and be found worthy to arrive with Mary
at the enjoyment
of Your eternal and blessed presence in heaven.
Amen.

## Prayer of Reparation

WITH the deep and humble feeling
that the Faith inspires in me,
O my God and Savior, Jesus Christ,
true God and true Man,
I love You with all my heart,
and I adore You Who are hidden here.

I do so in reparation
for all the irreverences, profanations, and sacrileges that You receive
in the most august Sacrament of the altar.

I adore You, O my God,
not so much as You are worthy to be adored,
nor so much as I am bound to do,
but at least as much as I am able.
Would that I could adore You
with the perfect worship
that the Angels in heaven are able to offer You.

O Jesus,
may You be known, adored, loved, and thanked
by all people at every moment
in this most holy and Divine Sacrament. Amen.

## Prayer of Thanksgiving and Petition

WE GIVE You thanks,
O Christ, our God;
in Your goodness
You have given us Your Body in this Sacrament
to enable us to live holy lives.
Through Your grace
keep us pure and without stain.
Remain in us to protect us.
Direct our steps in the way
of Your holy and benevolent Will.

Strengthen our souls
against the seductions of the devil
so that we may heed only Your voice
and follow You alone,
O omnipotent and truthful Shepherd,
and attain the place prepared for us
in the Kingdom of Heaven:
O our God and Lord,
Redeemer Jesus Christ,
Who are blessed

with the Father and the Spirit
now and forever. Amen.

## Prayer for Today's Needs

LORD, for tomorrow and its needs I do not pray;
keep me, my God, from stain of sin, just for today.
Let me both diligently work and duly pray;
let me be kind in word and deed, just for today.
Let me be slow to do my will, prompt to obey;
help me to mortify my flesh, just for today.
Let me no wrong or idle word unthinking say;
set a seal upon my lips, just for today.
Let me in season, Lord, be grave, in season gay;
let me be faithful to Your grace, just for today.
And if today my tide of life should ebb away,
give me Your Sacraments Divine, sweet Lord, today.
So for tomorrow and its needs, I do not pray;
but keep me, guide me, love me, Lord, just for today.

*Sister M. Xavier, S.N.D.*

## Prayer to Bring Christ into Our Day

LORD Jesus,
present before me in the Blessed Sacrament of the altar,
help me to cast out from my mind
all thoughts of which You do not approve
and from my heart
all emotions that You do not encourage.

Enable me to spend my entire day
as a coworker with You,
carrying out the tasks that You have entrusted to me.
Be with me at every moment of this day:

during the long hours of work,
that I may never tire or slacken from Your service;
during my conversations,
that they may not become for me
occasions for meanness toward others;
during the moments of worry and stress,
that I may remain patient and spiritually calm;
during periods of fatigue and illness,
that I may disregard self and think of others;
during times of temptation,
that I may take refuge in Your grace.

Help me to remain generous and loyal to You this day
and so be able to offer it all up to You
with its successes that I have achieved by Your help
and its failures that occurred
through my own fault.
Let me come to the wonderful realization
that life is most real
when it is lived with You as the Guest of my soul.
Amen.

## Hymn—Adoro Te

HIDDEN God, devoutly I adore You,
Truly present underneath these veils:
All my heart subdues itself before You,
Since it all before You faints and fails.

Not to sight, or taste, or touch be credit,
Hearing only do we trust secure;
I believe, for God the Son has said it—
Word of Truth that ever shall endure.

On the cross was veiled Your Godhead's splendor,
Here Your Manhood lies hidden too;
Unto both alike my faith I render,

And, as sued the contrite thief, I sue.
Though I look not on Your wounds with Thomas,
You, my Lord, and You, my God, I call:
Make me more and more believe Your promise,
Hope in You, and love You over all.

O memorial of my Savior dying,
Living Bread, that gives life to man;
Make my soul, its life from You supplying,

Taste Your sweetness, as on earth it can.
Deign, O Jesus, Pelican of heaven,
Me, a sinner, in Your Blood to lave,
To a single drop of which is given

All the world from all its sin to save.
Contemplating, Lord, Your hidden presence,
Grant me what I thirst for and implore,
In the revelation of Your essence
To behold Your glory evermore.

*St. Thomas Aquinas*

## Litany of the Blessed Sacrament
(For Private Devotion)

LORD, have mercy.
*Christ, have mercy.*
Lord, have mercy.
Christ, hear us.
*Christ, graciously hear us.*
God the Father of heaven, *have mercy on us.**
God the Son, Redeemer of the world,

* *Have mercy on us* is repeated after each invocation.

God the Holy Spirit,
Holy Trinity, one God,
Living Bread, that came down from heaven,
Hidden God and Savior,
Perpetual Sacrifice,
Clean Oblation,
Lamb without spot,
Most pure Feast,
Food of Angels,
Hidden Manna,
Memorial of the wonders of God,
Super-substantial Bread,
Word made flesh, dwelling in us,
Sacred Host,
Chalice of benediction,
Mystery of faith,
Most high and adorable Sacrament,
Most holy of all sacrifices,
True Propitiation for the living and the dead,
Heavenly Antidote against the poison of sin,
Most wonderful of all miracles,
Most holy Commemoration of the Passion of Christ,
Gift transcending all fullness,
Special Memorial of Divine love,
Affluence of Divine bounty,
Most august and holy Mystery,
Medicine of immortality,
Tremendous and life-giving Sacrament,
Bread made flesh by the omnipotence of the Word,
Unbloody Sacrifice,
Our Feast at once and our Fellow-guest,
Sweetest Banquet, at which Angels minister,
Sacrament of piety,

Bond of charity,
Priest and Victim,
Spiritual Sweetness tasted in its proper source,
Refreshment of holy souls,
Viaticum of such as die in the Lord,
Pledge of future glory,
Be merciful,
*spare us, O Lord.*
Be merciful,
*graciously hear us, O Lord.*
From an unworthy reception of Your Body and Blood,
*O Lord, deliver us.***
From the lust of the flesh,
From the lust of the eyes,
From the pride of life,
From every occasion of sin,
Through the desire, by which You desired to eat this Passover with Your disciples,
Through that profound humility, by which You washed their feet,
Through that ardent charity, by which You instituted this Divine Sacrament,
Through Your Precious Blood, that You have left us on our altars,
Through the Five Wounds of this Your most holy Body, that You received for us,
We sinners,
*we beseech You, hear us.****
That You would preserve and increase our faith, reverence, and devotion toward this admirable Sacrament,

** *O Lord, deliver us* is repeated after each invocation.
*** *We beseech You, hear us* is repeated after each invocation.

That You would conduct us, through a true confession of our sins, to a frequent reception of the holy Eucharist,
That You would deliver us from all heresy, perfidy, and blindness of heart,
That You would impart to us the precious and heavenly fruits of this most holy Sacrament,
That at the hour of death You would strengthen and defend us by this heavenly Viaticum,
Son of God,
Lamb of God, You take away the sins of the world;
*spare us, O Lord.*
Lamb of God, You take away the sins of the world;
*graciously hear us, O Lord.*
Lamb of God, You take away the sins of the world;
*have mercy on us.*
Christ, hear us.
*Christ, graciously hear us.*
℣. You gave them Bread from heaven,
℟. *Containing in Itself all sweetness.*

Let us pray.
O God,
in this wonderful Sacrament
You left us a memorial of Your Passion.
Grant us so to venerate the sacred mysteries
of Your Body and Blood
that we may ever continue to feel within us
the blessed fruit of Your Redemption.
You live and reign forever and ever. ℟. *Amen.*

# –11–

# Prayers from the Bible

## Prayers of Leaders and Kings

### Prayer of Moses

*Hymn of victory after the crossing of the Red Sea*

I will sing in honor of the Lord, for he is gloriously triumphant,
horse and horseman he has cast into the sea.
My strength and my song is the Lord,
for he has saved me.
He is my God, and I wish to praise him,
the God of my father, and I wish to exalt him.

The Lord is a warrior,
Lord is his name.
He has cast Pharaoh's chariots and his army into the sea.
His choice troops were drowned in the Red Sea.
At the breath of your nostrils, the waters piled up.
The flood waters piled up and stood like a mound;
the deep waters congealed in the midst of the sea.

The enemy had said, "I will pursue and overtake them.
I will divide the spoil, and my passion will be satisfied on them.
I will draw my sword, and my hand will destroy them."

You blew your wind, and the sea covered them.
Like lead they sank in the mighty waters.

Who is like you among the gods, O Lord?
Who is like you, majestic in holiness,
awesome in praise, doing wonders?
You extended your right hand
and the earth swallowed them.

In your mercy you guided the people you had redeemed.
You guided them with strength to your holy dwelling.
You will bring them in and plant them
on the mountain of your inheritance,
in the place that you have prepared for your dwelling, O Lord,
the sanctuary that your own hands have founded.
The Lord reigns forever and ever.

*Exodus 15:1-4a, 8-13, 17-18*

## Prayer of Hannah

*The humble find joy in God*

Then Hannah prayed and said,

"My heart rejoices in the Lord,
my horn is lifted high in the Lord.
My mouth boasts over my enemies,
for I rejoice in my salvation.
There is no holy one like the Lord,
there is none beside you,
nor is there a rock like our God.
Do not talk so proudly

nor let arrogance come forth from your mouth,
for the Lord is a knowing God,
and by him actions are weighed.

The bows of the mighty are broken,
the feeble are clothed in strength.
The well-fed hire themselves out for bread,
and the hungry cease to hunger.
The barren has borne seven times,
while she who has many children grows faint.

The Lord kills and brings to life.
He brings down to Sheol, and lifts up.
The Lord makes poor and makes rich,
he humbles and he also exalts.
He raises the poor from the dust,
and from the refuse he lifts up the beggar,
To seat them among princes,
that they might inherit a throne of glory.

For the Lord's are the pillars of the earth,
and he has set the world upon them.
He will guard the feet of his saints,
but the wicked will be cut off in the darkness,
for by strength none shall prevail.
Those who oppose the Lord will be shattered,
he will thunder against them from the heavens,
the Lord will judge the ends of the earth,
He will give strength to his king,
and exalt the horn of his anointed one."

*1 Samuel 2:1-10*

## Prayer of David

*Glory and honor are due to God*

David praised the Lord in front of the whole assembly, and David said:

"Blessed are you, O Lord,
the God of Israel,
our father forever and ever.

"Yours, O Lord, are greatness,
power, glory, strength, and majesty,
for everything in heaven and on earth is yours.
Yours, O Lord, is the kingdom;
you are exalted as head over all.
Wealth and honor are from you,
you reign over all.
In your hand are power and might;
it is in your hand to make great and to give strength to all.
Now, our God, we thank you,
and we praise your glorious name.
We are foreigners and aliens,
as all our fathers were before us.
Our days are like a shadow upon the earth,
none of them abide.
I know, my God,
that you have tested my heart,
and that you are pleased with
the integrity of my heart.
O Lord, God of our fathers,
of Abraham, Isaac, and Jacob,
keep this desire in the inner thoughts
of your people forever,
and make their hearts loyal to you.

*1 Chronicles 29:10-13, 15, 17a, 18*

# Prayers of Devout Individuals, Sages, and Prophets

## Prayer of Judith

*Refuge in God's almighty power*

Break into song to my God with tambourines,
sing to the Lord with cymbals.
Offer to him a psalm of praise,
exalt him and invoke his name.

I will sing a new hymn to my God.
O Lord, you are great and glorious,
wonderful in strength, invincible.
Let all your creatures serve you,
for you spoke and they were made.
You sent forth your spirit and they were created;
no one can resist your voice.
The mountains are shaken to their foundations;
at your glance the rocks melt like wax.

But to those who fear you
you still show compassion.

*Judith 16:1, 13-15*

## Prayer of Job

*The living God Who vindicates*

How I wish that my words might be written down
and inscribed on a scroll!
How I wish that with an iron chisel and with lead
they were engraved in stone forever!

But I know that my Redeemer lives,
and that at the end he will stand upon the dust.

After my awakening, he will call me close to him,
and then from my own flesh I will see God.

I know that you can do all things
and that no plan you conceive can be thwarted.
Because of my ignorance
I have spoken of things that I have not understood,
of things too wondrous for me to know.

I had heard of you only by hearsay,
but now that I have seen you with my own eyes,
I retract what I have said,
repenting in dust and ashes.

*Job 19:23-26, 42:2-6*

## Prayer of Sirach in Gratitude

*Prayer of thanksgiving for God's help*

I give thanks to you, O Lord and King,
and praise you, O God my Savior.
I give thanks to your name,
for you have been my protector and my support.

You have rescued me from destruction,
from the snare laid by a slanderous tongue,
and from lips that fabricate falsehood.
In the face of my adversaries you came to my aid;
I was surrounded on every side
and there was no one to help me.
I looked for human assistance
but there was none.
Then I remembered your mercy, O Lord,
and your kind deeds from the ages.

For you deliver those who put their trust in you
and rescue them from the power of their enemies.

Therefore, from the earth I sent up my plea,
begging to be rescued from death.
I cried out: "Lord, you are my Father,
and the champion of my salvation;
do not abandon me in my days of ordeal,
for I am helpless when confronted by the arrogant.
I will praise your name continually
and sing hymns of thanksgiving."

Thereupon my prayer was heard,
for you saved me from destruction
and delivered me from my desperate plight.
For this reason, I thank you and I praise you;
I bless the name of the Lord.

*Wisdom of Ben Sira 51:1-2, 7-12*

## Prayer of Isaiah

*Joy of God's ransomed people*

I will give you thanks, O Lord.
Even though you were angry with me,
your anger has abated
and you have consoled me.
God truly is my salvation;
I will trust in him and be unafraid.
For the Lord is my strength and my source of courage;
he has been my salvation.

With joy you will draw water
from the fountain of salvation,
and you will say on that day:

Give thanks to the Lord,
invoke his name;
make known his deeds among the nations;
proclaim that his name is exalted.

Sing praise to the Lord for his mighty deeds;
let this be known throughout the entire world.
Cry out and shout for joy,
all of you who dwell on Zion,
for great in your midst
is the Holy One of Israel.

*Isaiah 12:1-6*

## Prayer of Jeremiah

*The lament of the people in war and famine*

Let my eyes stream with tears
day and night without ceasing,
for my virgin daughter—my people—
has suffered a crushing blow
and is grievously injured.
If I go out into the open fields,
I see those slain by the sword.
If I go into the city,
I behold those who have perished through famine.
Even prophets and priests roam in confusion
in a land they do not know.

Have you rejected Judah completely?
Has Zion become loathsome to you?
Why have you afflicted us
to a point where we cannot be healed?
We hope for peace, but to no avail,
for a time of healing, only to encounter terror.

O Lord, we acknowledge our wickedness
  and the guilt of our fathers;
  we have indeed sinned against you.

For your name's sake do not reject us;
  do not dishonor your glorious throne.
Remember your covenant with us
  and do not break it.

*Jeremiah 14:17-21*

## Prayer of Habakkuk

*God comes to judge*

O Lord, I have heard of your renown;
  your work, O Lord, fills me with awe.
Make it live once again in our own time;
  in the course of the years make it known,
and in your wrath remember to have compassion on us.
You go forth to deliver your people,
  to save your anointed one.
You shatter the house of the wicked,
  laying bare its foundations to the bedrock.

I hear, and my body trembles;
  my lips quiver at the sound.
Decay afflicts my bones,
  and my legs tremble beneath me.
I wait calmly for the day of disaster
  that will dawn on the people who attack us.
Even though the fig tree does not blossom
  and there is no fruit on the vines,
even though the olive crop will fail
  and the orchards will yield no food,
even though the flock is cut off from the fold
  and there is no herd in the stalls,

I will continue to rejoice in the Lord,
and exult in the God of my salvation.
The Lord God is my strength;
he makes my feet as swift as those of a deer
and enables me to tread on the heights.

*Habakkuk 3:2, 13a, 16-19*

## Psalms—Prayer Book of the Spirit

### Prayer for True Happiness

*The way of the just*

Blessed is the man
who does not walk in the counsel of the wicked,
nor stand in the way of sinners,
nor sit in the company of scoffers.
Rather, his delight is in the law of the Lord,
and on that law he meditates day and night.

He is like a tree planted near streams of water,
which bears fruit in its season,
and whose leaves never wither.
In the same way,
everything he does will prosper.

This is not true of the wicked,
for they are like chaff that the wind blows away.
Therefore, the wicked will not stand firm at the judgment,
nor sinners in the assembly of the righteous.

For the Lord watches over the way of the righteous,
but the way of the wicked will perish.

*Psalm 1*

## Prayer of Extolling the Majesty of God and the Dignity of Humans

*Finite nature and infinite majesty*

O Lord, our Lord,
how glorious is your name in all the earth!
You have exalted your majesty above the heavens.
Out of the mouths of newborn babes and infants
you have brought forth praise
as a bulwark against your foes,
to silence the enemy and the avenger.

When I look up at your heavens
that have been formed by your fingers,
the moon and the stars
that you set in place,
what is man that you are mindful of him,
the son of man that you care for him?

You have made him a little less than the angels
and crowned him with glory and honor.

You have given him dominion over the works of your hands
and placed everything under his feet:
all sheep and oxen
as well as the beasts of the field,
the birds of the air, the fish of the sea,
and whatever swims in the paths of the sea.

O Lord, our Lord,
how glorious is your name in all the earth!

*Psalm 8*

## Prayer to the Good Shepherd

*Constant protector*

The Lord is my shepherd;
 there is nothing I shall lack.
He makes me lie down in green pastures;
 he leads me to tranquil streams.
He restores my soul,
 guiding me in paths of righteousness
 so that his name may be glorified.
Even though I wander
 through the valley of the shadow of death,
I will fear no evil,
 for you are at my side,
with your rod and your staff
 that comfort me.

You spread a table for me
 in the presence of my enemies.
You anoint my head with oil;
 my cup overflows.
Only goodness and kindness will follow me
 all the days of my life,
and I will dwell in the house of the Lord
 forever and ever.

*Psalm 23*

## Prayer in Time of Fear

*Trust in God*

The Lord is my light and my salvation;
 whom should I fear?
The Lord is the stronghold of my life;
 of whom should I be afraid?

When evildoers close in on me
 to devour my flesh,

it is they, my adversaries and enemies,
who stumble and fall.
Even if an army encamps against me,
my heart will not succumb to fear;
even if war breaks out against me,
I will not have my trust shaken.

There is only one thing I ask of the Lord,
just one thing I seek:
to dwell in the house of the Lord
all the days of my life,
so that I may enjoy the beauty of the Lord
and gaze on his temple.

For he will hide me in his shelter
in times of trouble.
He will conceal me under the cover of his tent
and place me high upon a rock.
Even now my head is raised high
above my enemies who surround me.
In his tent I will offer sacrifices with joyous shouts;
I will sing and chant praise to the Lord.

*Psalm 27:1-6*

## Prayer of Longing and Hope

*Longing to see God*

As a deer longs for running streams,
so my soul longs for you, O God.
My soul thirsts for God, the living God.
When shall I come to behold the face of God?

My tears have become my food
day and night,
while people taunt me all day long, saying,
"Where is your God?"

As I pour out my soul,
I recall those times
when I journeyed with the multitude
and led them in procession to the house of God,
amid loud cries of joy and thanksgiving
on the part of the crowd keeping festival.

Why are you so disheartened, O my soul?
Why do you sigh within me?
Place your hope in God,
for I will once again praise him,
my Savior and my God.

*Psalm 42:2-6*

## Prayer of Longing for God's Dwelling

*Longing for the sanctuary*

How lovely is your dwelling place,
O Lord of hosts.
My soul yearns and is filled with longing
for the courts of the Lord.
My heart and my flesh cry out
for the living God.

Just as the sparrow searches for a home
and the swallow builds a nest for herself
where she may place her young,
so do I seek your altars,
O Lord of hosts, my King and my God.

Blessed are those who dwell in your house;
they offer continuous praise to you.

*Psalm 84:2-5*

## Prayer of Praise of God's Law

Blessed are those whose way is blameless,
who walk in accord with the law of the Lord.
Blessed are those who observe his statutes
and seek him with their whole heart.
They do nothing wrong;
they walk in his ways.

You have ordained
that your commands be diligently observed.
May my ways be steadfast
in the observance of your decrees.
Then I will never be put to shame
when I take note of all your precepts.

I will praise you in sincerity of heart
as I ponder your righteous judgments.
I will observe your decrees;
do not forsake me completely.

*Psalm 119:1-8*

## Prayer in Thanksgiving for God's Kindness

*Give thanks*

Give thanks to the Lord, for he is good,
for his love endures forever.
Give thanks to the God of gods,
for his love endures forever.
Give thanks to the Lord of lords,
for his love endures forever.

He alone works great wonders,
for his love endures forever.
In his wisdom he made the heavens,
for his love endures forever.
He spread out the earth upon the waters,
for his love endures forever.

He made the great lights,
  for his love endures forever.
He made the sun to rule over the day,
  for his love endures forever.
He made the moon and stars to rule the night,
  for his love endures forever.

The Lord remembered us in our wretched state,
  for his love endures forever.
He rescued us from our enemies,
  for his love endures forever.
He provides food to every creature,
  for his love endures forever.

Give thanks to the God of heaven,
  for his love endures forever.

*Psalm 136:1-9, 23-26*

## Prayer of Praise Offered by All Creation

*Let all creation praise God*

Praise God in his sanctuary;
  praise him in the firmament of his power.
Praise him for his awesome acts,
  praise him for his immeasurable greatness.

Praise him with the sound of the trumpet,
  praise him with the harp and lyre.
Praise him with tambourines and dancing,
  praise him with strings and flutes.
Praise him with clanging cymbals,
  praise him with crashing cymbals.

Let everything that breathes
  offer praise to the Lord.
Alleluia.

*Psalm 150*

# Prayers from the Gospels

## Canticle of Mary

*The soul rejoices in the Lord*

My soul proclaims the greatness of the Lord
and my spirit rejoices in God my Savior.
For he has looked with favor on the lowliness of his servant;
henceforth all generations will call me blessed.
The Mighty One has done great things for me,
and holy is his name.
His mercy is shown from age to age
to those who fear him.
He has shown the strength of his arm,
he has routed those who are arrogant in the desires of their hearts.
He has brought down the mighty from their thrones
and lifted up the lowly.
He has filled the hungry with good things
and sent the rich away empty.
He has come to the aid of Israel his servant,
ever mindful of his merciful love,
according to the promises he made to our ancestors,
to Abraham and to his descendants forever.

*Luke 1:46-55*

## Canticle of Zechariah

*The Messiah and His forerunner*

Blessed be the Lord, the God of Israel,
for he has visited his people and redeemed them.

He has raised up a horn of salvation for us
from the house of his servant David,
just as he proclaimed through the mouth of his holy prophets from age to age:
salvation from our enemies and from the hands of all who hate us,
to show the mercy promised to our fathers
and to remain mindful of his holy covenant,
the oath that he swore to our father Abraham,
and to grant us that, delivered from the power of our enemies,
without fear we might worship him, in holiness and righteousness
in his presence all our days.
And you, my child, will be called prophet of the Most High,
for you will go before the Lord to prepare his ways,
to give his people knowledge of salvation
through the forgiveness of their sins,
because of the tender mercy of our God
by which the dawn from on high will break upon us
to shine on those who sit in darkness and in the shadow of death,
to guide our feet along the path of peace.

*Luke 1:68-79*

## Canticle of Simeon

*Christ is the light of the nations and the glory of Israel*

Now, Lord, you may dismiss your servant in peace,
according to your word;

for my eyes have seen your salvation,
which you have prepared in the sight of all the peoples,
a light of revelation to the Gentiles
and glory for your people Israel.

*Luke 2:29-32*

# Prayers from Pauline Epistles

## Praise of God's Wisdom and Knowledge

Oh, the depth of the riches and wisdom and knowledge of God!
How inscrutable are his judgments and how unfathomable his ways!
For who has known the mind of the Lord,
or who has been his counselor?
Or who has given him anything
in order to receive something in return?
For from him and through him and for him are all things.
To him be glory forever. Amen.

*Romans 11:33-36*

## Praise of Divine Love

If in speaking I use human tongues
and angelic as well,
but do not have love,
I am nothing more than a noisy gong or a clanging cymbal.
If I have the gift of prophecy
and the ability to understand all mysteries and all knowledge,

and have all the faith necessary to move mountains,
but do not have love,
I am nothing.
If I give away everything to feed the poor
and hand over my body to be burned,
but do not have love,
I achieve nothing.

Love is patient;
love is charitable.
Love is not envious;
it does not have an inflated opinion of itself;
it is not filled with its own importance.
Love is never rude;
it does not seek its own advantage.
It is not prone to anger;
neither does it brood over setbacks.
Love does not rejoice over wrongdoing
but rejoices in the truth.
Love bears all things,
believes all things,
hopes all things,
endures all things.
Love never fails.
Prophecies will eventually cease,
tongues will become silent,
and knowledge will pass away,
for our knowledge is partial
and our prophesying is partial;
but when we encounter what is perfect,
that which is imperfect will pass away.
When I was a child,
I used to talk like a child,
think like a child,

and reason like a child.
However, when I became a man,
I put all childish ways aside.
At the present time we see indistinctly, as in a mirror;
then we shall see face to face.
My knowledge is only partial now;
then I shall know fully,
even as I am fully known.
Thus there are three things that endure: faith, hope, and love,
and the greatest of these is love.

*1 Corinthians 13:1-13*

## Prayer to God Who Saves Us

Blessed be the God,
and Father of our Lord Jesus Christ,
who has blessed us in Christ
with every spiritual blessing in the heavens.
Before the foundation of the world
he chose us in Christ
to be holy and blameless in his sight
and to be filled with love.
He predestined us
for adoption as his children
through Jesus Christ,
in accordance with his purpose and pleasure,
to the praise of the glory
of his grace
that he so freely bestowed on us
in the Beloved.

In Christ
and through his blood
we have redemption

and the forgiveness of our sins.
In accord with the riches of his grace,
God lavished on us
all wisdom and insight.
He has made known to us
the mystery of his will
in accordance with his good pleasure
that he had predetermined in Christ
to be realized when
the fullness of time had been achieved:
namely, the plan to bring all things,
both in heaven and on earth,
together in Christ
as the head.

*Ephesians 1:3-10*

## Prayer for the Church

This is the reason why I kneel in prayer before the Father,
from whom every family in heaven and on earth takes its name.
I ask that from the riches of his glory
he may grant through his Spirit
that you be strengthened with power in your inner being
and that Christ may dwell in your hearts through faith.

And I pray that, rooted and grounded in love,
you may have the power to comprehend with all the saints
its breadth and length and height and depth,
and know Christ's love even though it is beyond knowledge,

so that you may be filled with all the fullness of God.

To him who in all things is able
through the power
that is at work within us
to accomplish abundantly far more
than all we can ask or imagine,
to him be glory in the Church
and in Christ Jesus
through all generations,
forever and ever. Amen.

*Ephesians 3:14-21*

## Prayer for Peace, Love, and Faith

May God the Father and the Lord Jesus Christ grant peace and love with faith to all the brethren.
Grace be with all
who love our Lord Jesus Christ
with undying devotion.

*Ephesians 6:23-24*

## Prayer of Thanksgiving to the Father

Give thanks to the Father who has enabled you to share in the inheritance of the saints in light.
He has rescued us from the power of darkness and brought us into the kingdom of his beloved Son,
in whom we have redemption, the forgiveness of sins.

He is the image of the invisible God,
the firstborn of all creation.

For in him were created all things
in heaven and on earth,
whether visible or invisible,
whether thrones or dominions or rulers or powers—
all things were created through him and for him.
He exists before all things,
and in him all things hold together.
He is the head of the body,
that is, the Church.
He is the beginning,
the firstborn from the dead,
so that in every way
He should be supreme.

For in him
it pleased God
to make all fullness dwell,
and through him
to reconcile all things for him,
whether on earth or in heaven,
by making peace through his blood of the cross.

*Colossians 1:12-20*

## Prayers from the Epistles

### God Is Light

This is the message
that we have heard from him
and that we declare to you:
God is light,
and there is no darkness at all in him.
If we claim that we have fellowship with him
while we continue to live in darkness,
we are lying and do not live in the truth.

However, if we live in the light
as he himself is in the light,
then we have fellowship with one another,
and the blood of Jesus his Son
purifies us from all sin.

If we claim that we are sinless,
we are only deceiving ourselves,
and the truth is not in us.
However, if we confess our sins,
he who is faithful and just
will forgive our sins
and cleanse us from all wrongdoing.
If we say that we have never sinned,
we make him out to be a liar,
and his word is not in us.

*1 John 1:5-10*

## The Commandment of Love

Now we may be certain that we know him
if we obey his commandments.
Whoever says, "I know him,"
but does not keep his commandments,
is a liar,
and the truth is not in him.
However, the love of God is truly perfected
in the one who obeys his word.
This is how we can be certain
that we are in union with him:
whoever claims to abide in him
must live just as he himself lived.

Beloved,
I am not writing a new commandment for you,
but an old commandment
that you have had from the beginning.

The old commandment is the word
that you have heard.
And yet I am writing you a new commandment,
whose truth is in him and in you,
because the darkness is passing away
and the true light is already shining.
Whoever says, "I am in the light,"
yet hates his brother,
is still in the darkness.
Whoever loves his brother lives in the light,
and there is nothing in him
to make him stumble.
Whoever hates his brother is in the darkness,
and he walks about in darkness.
He does not know where he is going
because the darkness has blinded him.

I am writing to you, dear children,
because your sins have been forgiven
on account of his name.
I am writing to you, fathers,
because you have known him
who has existed from the beginning.
I am writing to you, young people,
because you have conquered the evil one.
I am writing to you, dear children,
because you have known the Father.
I am writing to you, fathers,
because you have known him
who has existed from the beginning.
I am writing to you, young people,
because you are strong,
and the word of God abides in you,
and you have overcome the evil one.

Do not love the world
or what is in the world.
If anyone does love the world,
the love of the Father is not in him.
For everything that is in the world—
the concupiscence of the flesh,
the concupiscence of the eyes,
and the pride of life—
comes not from the Father
but from the world.
And the world with all its enticements
is passing away,
but whoever does the will of God
abides forever.

*1 John 2:3-17*

## Remain in Love

Beloved,
let us love one another,
because love is from God.
Everyone who loves is born of God
and knows God.
Whoever does not love
does not know God,
because God is love.
God's love was revealed to us
in this way:
God sent his only-begotten Son into the world
so that we might have life through him.
This is what love is:
not that we have loved God,
but that he loved us
and sent his Son as expiation for our sins.

*1 John 4:7-10*

Jesus in the Blessed Sacrament,
have mercy on us.

# PART IV
# CATHOLIC DEVOTIONS

## –1–

## Rite of Eucharistic Exposition and Benediction

WHEN the faithful adore Christ present in the sacrament, they should remember that this presence derives from the sacrifice and is directed toward both sacramental and spiritual Communion. In consequence, the devotion which leads the faithful to visit the Blessed Sacrament draws them into an ever deeper participation in the Paschal Mystery. It leads them to respond gratefully to the gift of Him Who through His humanity constantly pours divine life into the members of His Body. Dwelling with Christ our Lord, they enjoy His intimate friendship and pour out their hearts before Him for themselves and their dear ones, and pray for the peace and salvation of the world.

They offer their entire lives with Christ to the Father in the Holy Spirit, and receive in this wonderful exchange an increase of faith, hope, and charity. Thus they nourish those right dispositions which enable them with all due devotion to celebrate the memorial of the Lord and receive frequently the heavenly Bread, Christ truly present, given us by the Father.

## Down in Adoration Falling

DOWN in adoration falling,
Lo! the sacred Host we hail;
Lo! o'er ancient forms departing,
Newer rites of grace prevail;
Faith for all defects supplying,
Where the feeble senses fail.
To the everlasting Father,
And the Son Who reigns on high,
With the Holy Spirit proceeding
Forth from each eternally,
Be salvation, honor, blessing,
Might and endless majesty. Amen.

*The minister then says a prayer and concludes:*

For ever and ever.
℟. *Amen.*

## The Divine Praises

BLESSED be God.
Blessed be His holy Name.
Blessed be Jesus Christ, true God and true Man.
Blessed be the name of Jesus.
Blessed be His most Sacred Heart.
Blessed be His most Precious Blood.
Blessed be Jesus in the most holy Sacrament of the altar.
Blessed be the Holy Spirit, the Paraclete.
Blessed be the great Mother of God, Mary most holy.
Blessed be her holy and immaculate conception.
Blessed be her glorious assumption.
Blessed be the name of Mary,
virgin and mother.

Blessed be St. Joseph, her most chaste spouse.
Blessed be God in His Angels and in His Saints.

## Forty Hours Devotion

ALSO called Quarant' Ore or written in one word Quarantore, is a devotion in which continuous prayer is made for forty hours before the Blessed Sacrament exposed. It is commonly regarded as of the essence of the devotion that it should be kept up in a succession of churches, terminating in one at about the same hour at which it commences in the next.

A solemn high Mass, "Mass of Exposition," is sung at the beginning, and another, the "Mass of Deposition," at the end of the period of forty hours; and both these Masses are accompanied by a procession of the Blessed Sacrament and by the chanting of the litanies of the saints. The exact period of forty hours' exposition is not in practice very strictly adhered to; for the Mass of Deposition is generally sung, at about the same hour of the morning, two days after the Mass of Exposition. On the intervening day a solemn Mass *pro pace* is offered — if possible, at a different altar from the high altar upon which the Blessed Sacrament is exposed. It is assumed that the exposition and prayer should be kept up by night as well as by day, but permission is given to dispense with this requirement when an adequate number of watchers cannot be obtained. In such a case the interruption of the devotion by night does not forfeit the indulgences conceded by the Holy See to those who take part in it.

–2–

# Devotions to the Sacred Heart of Jesus

THE Heart of Jesus is the symbol of the infinite love that impelled the Son of God to become our brother, to die for us on the Cross, and to remain forever in the Sacrament of the Altar. Jesus asks each of us to return that love.

## The Promises of the Sacred Heart

In various appearances to St. Margaret Mary Alacoque, Jesus manifested His great love for human beings and made the following promises to those who give particular honor to His Sacred Heart.

1. I will give them all the graces necessary in their state of life.

2. I will establish peace in their homes.

3. I will comfort them in all their afflictions.

4. I will be their secure refuge during life, and above all in death.

5. I will bestow abundant blessings upon all their undertakings.

6. Sinners shall find in My Heart the source and the infinite ocean of mercy.

7. Tepid souls shall become fervent.

8. Fervent souls shall quickly mount to high perfection.

9. I will bless every place in which an image of My Heart shall be exposed and honored.

10. I will give to priests the gift of touching the most hardened hearts.

11. Those who shall promote this devotion shall have their names written in My Heart, never to be effaced.

12. I promise you in the excessive mercy of My Heart that My all-powerful love will grant to all those who communicate on the First Friday in nine consecutive months the grace of final penitence; they shall not die in My disgrace nor without receiving their Sacraments. My divine Heart shall be their safe refuge in this last moment.

## Prayer of Trust in the Sacred Heart

IN ALL my temptations, I place my trust in You, O Sacred Heart of Jesus.

In all my weaknesses, I place my trust in You, O Sacred Heart of Jesus.

In all my difficulties, I place my trust in You, O Sacred Heart of Jesus.

In all my trials, I place my trust in You, O Sacred Heart of Jesus.

In all my sorrows, I place my trust in You, O Sacred Heart of Jesus.

In all my work, I place my trust in You, O Sacred Heart of Jesus.

In every failure, I place my trust in You, O Sacred Heart of Jesus.

In every discouragement, I place my trust in You, O Sacred Heart of Jesus.

In life and in death, I place my trust in You,
O Sacred Heart of Jesus.
In time and in eternity, I place my trust in You,
O Sacred Heart of Jesus.

## Act of Dedication of the Human Race to Christ the King

MOST sweet Jesus, Redeemer of the human race, look down upon us humbly prostrate before You. We are Yours, and Yours we wish to be; but to be more surely united with You, behold, each one of us freely consecrates himself today to Your Most Sacred Heart.

Many indeed have never known You; many, too, despising Your precepts, have rejected You. Have mercy on them all, most merciful Jesus, and draw them to Your Sacred Heart.

Be King, O Lord, not only of the faithful who have never forsaken You, but also of the prodigal children who have abandoned You; grant that they may quickly return to their Father's house, lest they die of wretchedness and hunger.

Be King of those who are deceived by erroneous opinions, or whom discord keeps aloof, and call them back to the harbor of truth and the unity of faith, so that soon there may be but one flock and one Shepherd.

Grant, O Lord, to Your Church assurance of freedom and immunity from harm; give tranquility of order to all nations; make the earth resound from pole to pole with one cry: Praise to the divine Heart that wrought our salvation; to it be glory and honor forever. Amen.

*A* partial indulgence *is granted to the faithful, who piously recite the above Act of Dedication of the Human Race to Christ the King. A* plenary indulgence *is granted, if it is recited publicly on the feast of Christ the King.*

## Litany of the Most Sacred Heart of Jesus

LORD, have mercy.
*Christ, have mercy.*
Lord, have mercy.
Christ, hear us.
*Christ, graciously hear us.*
God, the Father of heaven,
*have mercy on us.**
God the Son, Redeemer of the world,
God, the Holy Spirit,
Holy Trinity, one God,
Heart of Jesus, Son of the eternal Father,
Heart of Jesus, formed by the Holy Spirit in the womb of the Virgin Mother,
Heart of Jesus, substantially united to the Word of God,
Heart of Jesus, of infinite majesty,
Heart of Jesus, sacred temple of God,
Heart of Jesus, tabernacle of the Most High,
Heart of Jesus, house of God and gate of heaven,
Heart of Jesus, burning furnace of love,
Heart of Jesus, abode of justice and love,
Heart of Jesus, full of goodness and love,
Heart of Jesus, abyss of all virtues,
Heart of Jesus, most worthy of all praise,
Heart of Jesus, King and center of all hearts,
Heart of Jesus, in Whom are all the treasures of wisdom and knowledge,

* *Have mercy on us* is repeated after each invocation.

Heart of Jesus, in Whom dwells the fullness of Divinity,
Heart of Jesus, in Whom the Father was well pleased,
Heart of Jesus, of Whose fullness we have all received,
Heart of Jesus, desire of the everlasting hills,
Heart of Jesus, patient and most merciful,
Heart of Jesus, enriching all who invoke You,
Heart of Jesus, fountain of life and holiness,
Heart of Jesus, propitiation for our sins,
Heart of Jesus, loaded down with disgrace,
Heart of Jesus, bruised for our offenses,
Heart of Jesus, obedient to death,
Heart of Jesus, pierced with a lance,
Heart of Jesus, source of all consolation,
Heart of Jesus, our life and resurrection,
Heart of Jesus, our peace and reconciliation,
Heart of Jesus, victim for our sins,
Heart of Jesus, salvation of those who trust in You,
Heart of Jesus, hope of those who die in You,
Heart of Jesus, delight of all the Saints,

Lamb of God, You take away the sins of the world; *spare us, O Lord.*
Lamb of God, You take away the sins of the world; *graciously hear us, O Lord.*
Lamb of God, You take away the sins of the world; *have mercy on us.*
℣. Jesus, meek and humble of heart.
℟. *Make our hearts like to Yours.*

Let us pray. Almighty and eternal God, look upon the Heart of Your most beloved Son and upon the praises and satisfaction which He offers You in the name of sinners; and to those who implore Your mercy, in Your great goodness, grant forgiveness in the name of the same Jesus Christ, Your Son, Who lives and reigns with You forever and ever.

## Prayer of Self-Offering to the Sacred Heart

O JESUS,
reveal Your Sacred Heart to me
and show me Its attractions.
Unite me to It forever.
Grant that all my desires and every beat of my heart,
which does not cease even while I sleep,
may be a witness to You of my love
and may say to You:
Yes, Lord, I am Yours!
The pledge of my loyalty to You
rests ever in my heart
and shall never cease to be there.

Accept the little good that I do
and be pleased to make up for all my wrongdoing,
so that I may be able to praise You in time
as well as in eternity.

## Prayer for Peace of Heart

O MOST sacred, most loving Heart of Jesus,
You are concealed in the Holy Eucharist,
and You beat for us still.
Now, as then, You say:
"With desire I have desired."
I worship You, then,
with all my best love and awe,
with fervent affection,

with my most subdued, most resolved will.
You for a while take up Your abode within me.
O make my heart beat with Your Heart!

Purify it of all that is earthly,
all that is proud and sensual,
all that is hard and cruel,
of all perversity,
of all disorder,
of all deadness.
So fill it with You,
that neither the events of the day,
nor the circumstances of the time,
may have the power to ruffle it;
but that in Your power and Your fear,
it may have peace. *St. John Newman*

## Prayer of Thanksgiving to the Father for Giving Us the Heart and Mind of Jesus

O MY God,
how great is Your love for us!
You are infinitely worthy
of being loved, praised, and glorified!
We have neither heart nor spirit worthy of doing so.
But Your Wisdom and Goodness
have given us a way of carrying it out.
You have given us the Spirit and Heart of Your Son,
to be our own heart and spirit,
in accord with the promise You made through Your Prophet:
"I will give them a new heart,
I will put a new spirit in your midst" (Ezek 36:26).
In order that we may know

what this new heart and new spirit might be
You added:
"I will put My Spirit, which is My Heart,
in Your midst."
Only the Spirit and Heart of a God
are worthy of loving and praising a God,
of blessing and loving Him as much as He deserves.
Thus You have given us Your Heart,
the Heart of Your Son Jesus,
as well as the heart of His holy Mother
and the heart of the Saints, and Angels,
who together are only one heart,
as the Head and members form one single Body.

*St. John Eudes*

## Petitions to the Sacred Heart of Jesus

LOVE of the Sacred Heart of Jesus,
embrace my heart.
Fire of the Heart of Jesus, inflame my heart.
Charity of the Heart of Jesus, fill my heart.
Strength of the Heart of Jesus, sustain my heart.
Mercy of the Heart of Jesus, pardon my heart.
Patience of the Heart of Jesus, do not forsake my heart.
Reign of the Heart of Jesus, establish Yourself in my heart.
Wisdom of the Heart of Jesus, teach my heart.
Will of the Heart of Jesus, guide my heart.
Zeal of the Heart of Jesus, consume my heart.

## Prayer of Adoration and Petition

MOST holy Heart of Jesus,
fountain of every blessing,
I love You.

With a lively sorrow for my sins
I offer You this poor heart of mine.
Make me humble, patient, and pure,
and perfectly obedient to Your Will.

Good Jesus,
grant that I may live in You and for You.
Protect me in the midst of danger
and comfort me in my afflictions.
Bestow on me health of body,
assistance in temporal needs,
Your blessing on all that I do,
and the grace of a holy death.

## Prayer for Perseverance

O SACRED Heart of Jesus,
living and life-giving fountain of eternal life,
infinite treasure of the Divinity,
and glowing furnace of love,
You are my refuge and my sanctuary.
O adorable and glorious Savior,
consume my heart with the burning fire
that ever inflames Your Heart.
Pour down on my soul the graces
that flow from Your love.
Let my heart be so united with Yours
that our wills may be one,
and mine may in all things be conformed to Yours.
May Your Will be the rule
both of my desires and of my actions

*St. Alphonsus Liguori*

## Contemporary Prayer of Reparation

LORD Jesus Christ,
we look at the Cross,

and we—Your pilgrim Church—can see
what sin has done to the Son of Mary,
to the Son of God.

But now You are risen and glorified.
You suffer no more in the flesh.
Sin can no longer expose You
to the Agony of the Garden,
to the Scourging,
to Death on a Cross.

But it can reach You through Your Mystical Body.
This part of You, Your Church on earth,
still feels the strength of sin.

For this we make our act of reparation.
We who have sinned in the past
now consecrate ourselves
to the healing of Your Mystical Body,
to our part in the mystery
of its well-being and its growth.
Sanctify us for this task.

May Your Sacred Heart be the symbol,
not of one love but two—
Your love for us and ours for You.
Accept our love, and help us make it real
by serving You in our brothers and sisters,
so that love and concern may lead all people
"to know the one true God
and Jesus Christ Whom He has sent."

*Apostleship of Prayer*

## Prayer of Consecration

I, *N . . .*, GIVE myself
to the Sacred Heart of our Lord Jesus Christ,

and I consecrate to Him
my person and my life,
my actions, pains, and sufferings,
so that henceforth I shall be unwilling
to make use of any part of my being
except for the honor, love, and glory
of the Sacred Heart.

My unchanging purpose is to be all His
and to do all things for the love of Him
while renouncing with all my heart
whatever is displeasing to Him.

I take You, O Sacred Heart,
as the only object of my love,
the guardian of my life,
the assurance of my salvation,
the remedy of my weakness and inconstancy,
the atonement for all my faults,
and the sure refuge at my death.

O Heart of goodness,
be my justification before God the Father,
and turn away from me
the strokes of His righteous anger.
O Heart of love,
I place all my trust in You,
for I fear everything
from my own wickedness and frailty,
but I hope for all things
from Your goodness and bounty.

Consume in me all that can displease You
or resist Your holy Will.
Let Your pure love imprint You
so deeply upon my heart
that I shall nevermore be able to forget You

or be separated from You.
May I obtain from all Your loving kindness
the grace of having my name written in You,
for I desire to place in You
all my happiness and all my glory,
living and dying in virtual bondage to You.

*St. Margaret Mary Alacoque*

## Prayer of Family Consecration

SACRED Heart of Jesus,
You revealed to St. Margaret Mary
Your desire to reign over Christian families.
To fulfill this desire we today proclaim
Your complete dominion over our family.
From now on we wish to live Your life,
to cultivate in our home
those virtues which bring them Your peace,
and avoid that worldliness which You have condemned.
You will rule over our minds by simple faith
and over our hearts by a love
kept aflame by frequent Holy Communion.

Divine Heart of Jesus,
be pleased to preside over our family,
to bless all we do,
to dispel our troubles,
sanctify our joys,
lighten our sufferings.
If one of us should ever offend You by sin,
remind him/her,
merciful Jesus,
of Your goodness and mercy to the penitent sinner.
And when the hour of separation strikes,
when death brings its griefs into our midst,

those of us who go and those who must stay
will be submissive to what You have decreed.

Then it will be our consolation to remember
that the day will come when our entire family,
reunited in heaven,
will be able to sing forever
of Your glory and Your mercy.

May the Immaculate Heart of Mary
and the glorious patriarch St. Joseph
present to You this Consecration of ours
and keep us ever mindful of it
all the days of our life.
All glory to the Sacred Heart of Jesus,
our King and our Father!

*American Apostleship of Prayer*

## Traditional Morning Offering

O JESUS,
through the Immaculate Heart of Mary,
I offer You my prayers, works, joys, and sufferings
of this day
in union with the Holy Sacrifice of the Mass
throughout the world.
I offer them
for all the intentions of Your Sacred Heart:
the salvation of souls,
reparation for sins,
the reunion of all Christians.

I offer them for the intentions of our Bishops
and of all the Apostles of Prayer,
and in particular for those
recommended by our Holy Father for this month.

*Apostleship of Prayer*

## Contemporary Morning Offering

ETERNAL Father,
I offer You everything I do this day:
my work, my prayers, my apostolic efforts;
my time with family and friends;
my hours of relaxation;
my difficulties, problems, distress,
which I shall try to bear with patience.

Join these my gifts to the unique offering
which Jesus Christ, Your Son, renews today
in the Eucharist.

Grant, I pray, that,
vivified by the Holy Spirit
and united to the Sacred Heart of Jesus,
my life this day may be of service
to You and to Your children
and help consecrate the world to You.

*Apostleship of Prayer*

## Invocations in Honor of the Sacred Heart

MAY the Sacred Heart of Jesus
be loved everywhere.

SWEET Heart of my Jesus,
grant that I may ever love You more.

SACRED Heart of Jesus,
Your Kingdom come!

DIVINE Heart of Jesus,
convert sinners,
save the dying,
and deliver the holy souls in purgatory.

SACRED Heart of Jesus,
I believe in Your love for me.

GLORY, love and thanksgiving
be to the Sacred Heart of Jesus!

O HEART of love,
I put all my trust in You;
for I fear all things from my weakness,
but I hope for all things from Your goodness.

SACRED Heart of Jesus,
have mercy on us
and on our erring brothers and sisters.

SACRED Heart of Jesus,
may You be known, loved, and imitated!

SACRED Heart of Jesus,
protect our families.

SACRED Heart of Jesus,
strengthened in Your Agony by an Angel,
strengthen us in our agony.

SACRED Heart of Jesus,
let me love You and make You loved.

SACRED Heart of Jesus,
grant that peace,
the fruit of justice and charity,
may reign throughout the world.

–3–

# Devotions to the Precious Blood

## Litany of the Precious Blood

LORD, have mercy.
*Christ have mercy.*
Lord, have mercy.
Christ, hear us.
*Christ, graciously hear us.*
God, the Father of heaven, have mercy on us.
God the Son, Redeemer of the world,
*have mercy on us.*
God, the Holy Spirit,
*have mercy on us.*
Holy Trinity, one God,
*have mercy on us.*

Blood of Christ, only-begotten Son of the eternal Father, *save us.* *
Blood of Christ, incarnate Word of God,
Blood of Christ, of the new and eternal Testament,
Blood of Christ, falling upon the earth in the Agony,
Blood of Christ, shed profusely in the Scourging,
Blood of Christ, flowing forth in the Crowning with Thorns,
Blood of Christ, poured out on the Cross,
Blood of Christ, price of our salvation,
Blood of Christ, without which there is no forgiveness,
Blood of Christ, Eucharistic drink and refreshment of souls,

* *Save us* is repeated after each invocation.

Blood of Christ, stream of mercy,
Blood of Christ, victor over demons,
Blood of Christ, courage of Martyrs,
Blood of Christ, strength of Confessors,
Blood of Christ, bringing forth Virgins,
Blood of Christ, help of those in peril,
Blood of Christ, relief of the burdened,
Blood of Christ, solace in sorrow,
Blood of Christ, hope of the penitent,
Blood of Christ, consolation of the dying,
Blood of Christ, peace and tenderness of hearts,
Blood of Christ, pledge of eternal life,
Blood of Christ, freeing souls from purgatory,
Blood of Christ, most worthy of all glory and honor,

Lamb of God, You take away the sins of the world; *spare us, O Lord!*

Lamb of God, You take away the sins of the world; *graciously hear us, O Lord!*

Lamb of God, You take away the sins of the world; *have mercy on us.*

℣. You have redeemed us, O Lord, in Your Blood.
℟. *And made us, for our God, a kingdom.*

## Prayer of Offering of the Precious Blood

ETERNAL Father,
You have given Your only Son
to be the Redeemer of the world
and willed that He should shed—
even to the last drop—
His Precious Blood for love of all persons.

I offer You
the effusion of the Precious Blood,

Which flowed beneath the knife of the circumcision,
Which watered the Garden of Olives,
Which flooded the praetorium and streets of Jerusalem,
Which was shed in torrents at the Crucifixion,
and Whose last drops reddened the steel of the lance.

In the name of this adorable Blood,
grant to sinners the grace of salvation,
to the just an increase of love,
and to all human beings a large share
in the merits that It has assured us.
Pardon us in the name of this Divine Blood.
Heed Its pleading voice.
Remember that It is the Blood of Your Son
in Whose Name You have promised to hear
our every prayer.

## Petitions in Honor of the Precious Blood

PRECIOUS Blood of Jesus,
shed in the Circumcision,
make me pure of mind, heart, and body.

PRECIOUS Blood,
oozing from every pore of Jesus in the Agony,
enable me to love God's holy Will above all.

PRECIOUS Blood,
flowing abundantly in the Scourging at the Pillar,
inspire me with a keen sorrow for my sins,
and a high-level tolerance of suffering.

PRECIOUS Blood,
falling in profusion from the Crown of Thorns,
grant me a ready acceptance of humiliations.

PRECIOUS Blood,
shed so profusely in the Crucifixion of our Lord,
make me die entirely to self-love.

PRECIOUS Blood,
shed to the very last drop
by the opening of Christ's Sacred Heart,
give me the generous love
that sacrifices all for God.

PRECIOUS Blood,
sacred price of my redemption,
apply to me Your infinite merits.

PRECIOUS Blood of Jesus,
I adore You from the depths of my heart;
I invoke You ardently
for You are my salvation,
and by You I hope to obtain the joys of heaven.

## Prayer of Intercession

ETERNAL Father,
I offer You the merits of the Precious Blood
of Your beloved Son Jesus, my Savior and my God,
for the spread and exaltation of the Church,
the welfare of her visible Head, the Pope,
the Bishops and pastors of souls,
and all the ministers of the sanctuary.

Blessed and praised for evermore be Jesus,
Who saved us with His Blood.

Eternal Father,
I offer You the merits of the Precious Blood
of Your beloved Son Jesus, my Savior and my God,

for peace and concord among nations,
the humbling of the enemies of the Faith,
and the welfare of all Christian people.

Blessed and praised for evermore be Jesus,
Who saved us with His Blood.

Eternal Father,
I offer You the merits of the Precious Blood
of Your beloved Son Jesus, my Savior and my God,
for the conversion of unbelievers,
the elimination of all heresies,
and the return of sinners.

Blessed and praised for evermore be Jesus,
Who saved us with His Blood.

Eternal Father,
I offer You the merits of the Precious Blood
of Your beloved Son Jesus, my Savior and my God,
for all my relatives, friends, and enemies,
for all in need, sickness, or tribulation,
for all those for whom You know I am bound to pray,
for all those for whom You know and desire that I should pray.

Blessed and praised for evermore be Jesus,
Who saved us with His Blood.

Eternal Father,
I offer You the merits of the Precious Blood
of Your beloved Son Jesus, my Savior and my God,
for all who are to depart from life this day,
that You would deliver them from the pains of hell,

and admit them speedily to the possession
of Your glory.

Blessed and praised for evermore be Jesus,
Who saved us with His Blood.

Eternal Father,
I offer You the merits of the Precious Blood
of Your beloved Son Jesus, my Savior and my God,
for all who love this great treasure
and who join me in adoring and glorifying It
and who labor to spread this devotion.

Blessed and praised for evermore be Jesus,
Who saved us with His Blood.

Eternal Father,
I offer You the merits of the Precious Blood
of Your beloved Son Jesus, my Savior and my God,
for all my needs both temporal and spiritual,
as an intercession for the faithful departed,
and in a special manner for those
who were most devoted to this price of our redemption,
and to the sorrows and sufferings of our Mother, Mary most holy.

Blessed and praised for evermore be Jesus,
Who saved us with His Blood.

Glory to the Blood of Jesus
both now and for evermore
and through the everlasting ages.

## Invocations in Honor of the Precious Blood

ETERNAL Father,
I offer You the most Precious Blood of Jesus
in atonement for my sins,
in supplication for the faithful departed,
and for the needs of holy Church.

BE MINDFUL, O Lord, of Your creature,
whom You have redeemed by Your Precious Blood.

HAIL, Precious Blood,
flowing from the wounds
of our crucified Lord Jesus Christ
and washing away the sins of the whole world!

PRECIOUS Blood of Jesus,
cleanse and purify all sinners.

PRECIOUS Blood of Jesus,
may Your powerful voice drive far from us
all the scourges that threaten us.

PRECIOUS Blood of Jesus,
by You may reparation be offered to the glory of God.

BLESSED be the Precious Blood of Jesus,
Which renders bearable the thorns of earth,
redeems our souls,
purifies them from their inequities,
and prepares them for an eternal crown.

## –4–

# The Way of the Cross

*Kneeling before the altar, make an Act of Contrition, and form the intention of gaining the indulgences, whether for yourself or for the souls in Purgatory.*

Then say:

MY LORD Jesus Christ, You have made this journey to die for me with love unutterable, and I have so many times unworthily abandoned You; but now I love You with my whole heart, and because I love You, I repent sincerely for having ever offended You. Pardon me, my God, and permit me to accompany You on this journey. * You go to die for love of me; I wish also, my beloved Redeemer, to die for love of You. My Jesus, I will live and die always united to You.

*Dear Jesus, You go to die*
*for very love of me.*
*Let me bear You company;*
*I wish to die with You.*

## 1. JESUS IS CONDEMNED TO DEATH

℣. We adore You, O Christ, and we bless You.
℟. *Because by Your holy Cross, You have redeemed the world.*

Consider how Jesus, after having been scourged and crowned with thorns, was unjustly condemned by Pilate to die on the Cross.

MY JESUS, it was not Pilate, no, it was my sins that condemned You to die. I beg You, by the merits of this sorrowful journey, to assist my soul in its journey toward eternity. I love You, my beloved Jesus; I love You more than myself; I repent with my whole heart for having offended You. Never permit me to separate myself from You again. Grant that I may love You always; and then do with me what You will.

*Our Father, Hail Mary, Glory Be*

At the Cross her station keeping,
stood the mournful Mother weeping,
close to Jesus to the last.

## 2. JESUS CARRIES HIS CROSS

℣. We adore You, O Christ, and we bless You.
℟. *Because by Your holy Cross, You have redeemed the world.*

Consider how Jesus, in making this journey with the Cross on His shoulders, thought of us, and for us offered to His Father the death He was about to undergo.

MY BELOVED Jesus, I embrace all the tribulations You have destined for me until death. I beg You, by the merits of the pain You suffered in carrying Your Cross, to give me the necessary help to carry mine with perfect patience and resignation. I love You, Jesus, my love; I repent of having offended You. Never permit me to separate myself from You again. Grant that I may love You always; and then do with me what You will.

*Our Father, Hail Mary, Glory Be*

Through her heart, His sorrow sharing,
all His bitter anguish bearing,
now at length the sword had passed!

## 3. JESUS FALLS THE FIRST TIME

℣. We adore You, O Christ, and we bless You.
℟. *Because by Your holy Cross, You have redeemed the world.*

Consider this first fall of Jesus under His Cross. His flesh was torn by the scourges, His head crowned with thorns, and He had lost a great quantity of blood. He was so weakened that He could scarcely walk, and yet He had to carry this great load upon His shoulders. The soldiers struck Him rudely, and thus He fell several times in His journey.

MY BELOVED Jesus, it is not the weight of the Cross, but my sins, which have made You suffer so much pain. By the merits of this first fall, deliver me from the misfortune of falling into mortal sin. I love You, O my Jesus, with my whole heart; I repent of having offended You. Never permit me to offend You again. Grant that I may love You always; and then do with me what You will.

*Our Father, Hail Mary, Glory Be*

O, how sad, and sore distressed,
was that Mother, highly blest,
of the sole-begotten One.

## 4. JESUS MEETS HIS MOTHER

℣. We adore You, O Christ, and we bless You.
℟. *Because by Your holy Cross, You have redeemed the world.*

Consider the meeting of the Son and the Mother, which took place on this journey. Jesus and Mary looked at each other, and their looks became as so many arrows to wound those hearts which loved each other so tenderly.

MY MOST loving Jesus, by the sorrow You experienced in this meeting, grant me the grace of a truly devoted love for Your most holy Mother. And you, my Queen, who were overwhelmed with sorrow, obtain for me by your intercession a continual remembrance of the Passion of your Son. I love You, Jesus, my love; I repent of ever having offended You. Never permit me to offend You again. Grant that I may love You always; and then do with me what You will.

*Our Father, Hail Mary, Glory Be*

Christ above in torment hangs,
she beneath beholds the pangs
of her dying, glorious Son.

## 5. SIMON HELPS JESUS TO CARRY THE CROSS

℣. We adore You, O Christ, and we bless You.
℟. *Because by Your holy Cross, You have redeemed the world.*

Consider how the Jews, seeing that at each step Jesus from weakness was on the point of expiring, and fearing that He would die on the way, when they wished Him to die the ignominious death of the Cross, constrained Simon the Cyrenian to carry the Cross behind our Lord.

MY BELOVED Jesus, I will not refuse the Cross, as the Cyrenian did; I accept it, I embrace it. I accept in particular the death You have destined for me; with all the pains that may accompany it; I unite it to Your Death, I offer it to You. You have died for love of me; I will die for love of You and to please You. Help me by Your grace. I love You, Jesus, my love; I repent of having offended You. Never permit me to offend You again. Grant that I may love You always; and then do with me what You will.

*Our Father, Hail Mary, Glory Be*

Is there one who would not weep,
whelmed in miseries so deep,
Christ's dear Mother to behold?

## 6. VERONICA WIPES THE FACE OF JESUS

℣. We adore You, O Christ, and we bless You.
℟. *Because by Your holy Cross, You have redeemed the world.*

Consider how the holy woman named Veronica, seeing Jesus so afflicted, and His face bathed in sweat and blood, presented Him with a towel, with which He wiped His adorable face, leaving on it the impression of His holy countenance.

MY BELOVED Jesus, Your face was beautiful before, but in this journey it has lost all its beauty, and wounds and blood have disfigured it. My soul also was once beautiful, when it received Your grace in Baptism; but I have disfigured it since by my sins; You alone, my Redeemer, can restore it to its former beauty. Do this by Your Passion; O Jesus. I repent of having offended You. Never permit me to offend You again. Grant that I may love You always; and then do with me what You will.

*Our Father, Hail Mary, Glory Be*

Can the human heart refrain
from partaking in her pain,
in that Mother's pain untold?

## 7. JESUS FALLS THE SECOND TIME

℣. We adore You, O Christ, and we bless You.
℟. *Because by Your holy Cross, You have redeemed the world.*

Consider the second fall of Jesus under the Cross—a fall which renews the pain of all the wounds of the head and members of our afflicted Lord.

MY MOST gentle Jesus, how many times You have pardoned me, and how many times have I fallen again, and begun again to offend You! By the merits of this new fall, give me the necessary help to persevere in Your grace until death. Grant that in all temptations which assail me I may always commend myself to You. I love You, Jesus my love, with my whole heart; I repent of having offended You. Never permit me to offend You again. Grant that I may love You always; and then do with me what You will.

*Our Father, Hail Mary, Glory Be*

Bruised, derided, cursed, defiled,
she beheld her tender Child
all with bloody scourges rent.

## 8. JESUS MEETS THE WOMEN OF JERUSALEM

℣. **We adore You, O Christ, and we bless You.**
℟. ***Because by Your holy Cross, You have redeemed the world.***

**Consider how those women wept with compassion at seeing Jesus in such a pitiable state, streaming with blood, as He walked along. But Jesus said to them: "Weep not for Me, but for your children."**

**MY JESUS, laden with sorrows, I weep for the offenses I have committed against You, because of the pains they have deserved, and still more because of the displeasure they have caused You, Who have loved me so much. It is Your love, more than the fear of hell, which causes me to weep for my sins. My Jesus, I love You more than myself; I repent of having offended You. Never permit me to offend You again. Grant that I may love You always; and then do with me what You will.**

*Our Father, Hail Mary, Glory Be*

**For the sins of His own nation,**
**saw Him hang in desolation,**
**till His spirit forth He sent.**

## 9. JESUS FALLS THE THIRD TIME

℣. **We adore You, O Christ, and we bless You.**
℟. ***Because by Your holy Cross, You have redeemed the world.***

**Consider the third fall of Jesus Christ. His weakness was extreme, and the cruelty of His executioners excessive, who tried to hasten His steps when He had scarcely strength to move.**

**MY OUTRAGED Jesus, by the merits of the weakness You suffered in going to Calvary, give me strength sufficient to conquer all human respect, and all my wicked passions, which have led me to despise Your friendship. I love You, Jesus my love, with my whole heart; I repent of having offended You. Never permit me to offend You again. Grant that I may love You always; and then do with me what You will.**

*Our Father, Hail Mary, Glory Be*

**O thou Mother! fount of love!**
**Touch my spirit from above,**
**make my heart with thine accord.**

## 10. JESUS IS STRIPPED OF HIS GARMENTS

℣. We adore You, O Christ, and we bless You.
℟. *Because by Your holy Cross, You have redeemed the world.*

Consider the violence with which the executioners stripped Jesus. His inner garments adhered to His torn flesh, and they dragged them off so roughly that the skin came with them. Compassionate your Savior thus cruelly treated, and say to Him:

MY INNOCENT Jesus, by the merits of the torment You have felt, help me to strip myself of all affection to things of earth, in order that I may place all my love in You, Who are so worthy of my love. I love You, Jesus, with my whole heart; I repent of having offended You. Never permit me to offend You again. Grant that I may love You always; and then do with me what You will.

*Our Father, Hail Mary, Glory Be*

Make me feel as thou hast felt.
Make my soul to glow and melt
with the love of Christ my Lord.

## 11. JESUS IS NAILED TO THE CROSS

℣. We adore You, O Christ, and we bless You.
℟. *Because by Your holy Cross, You have redeemed the world.*

Consider how Jesus, after being thrown on the Cross, extended His hands, and offered to His Eternal Father the sacrifice of His Death for our salvation. These barbarians fastened Him with nails, and then, raising the Cross, allowed Him to die with anguish on this infamous gibbet.

MY JESUS! loaded with contempt, nail my heart to Your feet, that it may ever remain there, to love You, and never leave You again. I love You more than myself; I repent of having offended You. Never permit me to offend You again. Grant that I may love You always; and then do with me what You will.

*Our Father, Hail Mary, Glory Be*

Holy Mother! pierce me through.
In my heart each wound renew
of my Savior Crucified.

## 12. JESUS DIES ON THE CROSS

℣. We adore You, O Christ, and we bless You.
℟. *Because by Your holy Cross, You have redeemed the world.*

Consider how your Jesus, after hours of Agony on the Cross, consumed at length with anguish, abandons Himself to the weight of His body, bows His head, and dies.

O MY dying Jesus, I kiss devoutly the Cross on which You died for love of me. I have merited by my sins to die a miserable death; but Your Death is my hope. By the merits of Your Death, give me grace to die, embracing Your feet, and burning with love for You. I yield my soul into Your hands. I love You with my whole heart; I repent of ever having offended You. Never permit me to offend You again. Grant that I may love You always; and then do with me what You will.

*Our Father, Hail Mary, Glory Be*

Let me share with thee His pain,
Who for all my sins was slain,
Who for me in torments died.

## 13. JESUS IS TAKEN DOWN FROM THE CROSS

℣. We adore You, O Christ, and we bless You.
℟. *Because by Your holy Cross, You have redeemed the world.*

Consider how, after the Death of our Lord, two of His disciples, Joseph and Nicodemus, took Him down from the Cross, and placed Him in the arms of His afflicted Mother, who received Him with unutterable tenderness, and pressed Him to her bosom.

O MOTHER of sorrow, for the love of this Son, accept me for your servant, and pray to Him for me. And You, my Redeemer, since You have died for me, permit me to love You; for I desire only You, and nothing more. I love You, my Jesus, and I repent of ever having offended You. Never permit me to offend You again. Grant that I may love You always; and then do with me what You will.

*Our Father, Hail Mary, Glory Be*

Let me mingle tears with thee,
mourning Him who mourned for me,
all the days that I may live.

## 14. JESUS IS LAID IN THE TOMB

℣. We adore You, O Christ, and we bless You.
℟. *Because by Your holy Cross, You have redeemed the world.*

Consider how the disciples carried the body of Jesus to bury it, accompanied by His holy Mother, who arranged it in the sepulcher with her own hands. They then closed the tomb, and all withdrew.

O MY buried Jesus, I kiss the stone that encloses You. But You rose again the third day. I beg You, by Your Resurrection, make me rise glorious with You at the last day, to be always united with You in heaven, to praise You and love You forever. I love You, and I repent of ever having offended You. Never permit me to offend You again. Grant that I may love You always; and then do with me what You will.

*Our Father, Hail Mary, Glory Be*

By the Cross with thee to stay,
there with thee to weep and pray,
is all I ask of thee to give.

–5–

# Devotions to the Holy Trinity

## Prayer of Consecration

O EVERLASTING and Triune God,
I consecrate myself wholly to You today.
Let all my days offer You ceaseless praise,
my hands move to the rhythm of Your impulses,
my feet be swift in Your service,
my voice sing constantly of You,
my lips proclaim Your message,
my eyes perceive You everywhere,
and my ears be attuned to Your inspirations.
May my intellect be filled with Your wisdom,
my will be moved by Your beauty,
my heart be enraptured with Your love,
and my soul be flooded with Your grace.
Grant that every action of mine be done
for Your greater glory
and the advancement of my salvation.

## Prayer in Praise of the Trinity

I VENERATE and glorify You,
O most Blessed Trinity,
in union with that ineffable glory
with which God the Father,
in His omnipotence,
honors the Holy Spirit forever.

I magnify and bless You,
O most Blessed Trinity
in union with that most reverent glory
with which God the Son,

in His unsearchable wisdom,
glorifies the Father and the Holy Spirit forever.

I adore and extol You,
O most Blessed Trinity,
in union with that most adequate and befitting glory
with which the Holy Spirit,
in His unchangeable goodness,
extols the Father and the Son forever.

## The Glory Be

GLORY to the Father,
and to the Son,
and to the Holy Spirit.
As it was in the beginning,
is now, and will be forever.

## Litany of the Most Holy Trinity

(For Private Devotion)

LORD, have mercy.
*Christ, have mercy.*
Lord, have mercy.
Blessed Trinity, hear us.
*Adorable Unity, graciously hear us.*
God the Father of heaven,
*have mercy on us.*
God the Son, Redeemer of the world,*
God the Holy Spirit,
Holy Trinity, one God,
Father, from Whom are all things,
Son, through Whom are all things,
Holy Spirit, in Whom are all things,
Holy and undivided Trinity,

* *Have mercy on us* is repeated after each invocation.

Father everlasting,
Only-begotten Son of the Father.
Spirit, Who proceed from the Father and the Son,
Co-eternal Majesty of Three Divine Persons,
Father the Creator,
Son the Redeemer,
Holy Spirit the Comforter,
Holy, holy, holy Lord God of hosts,
Who are, Who were, and Who are to come,
God, Most High, Who inhabit eternity,
To Whom alone are due all honor and glory,
Who alone do great wonders,
Power infinite,
Wisdom incomprehensible,
Love unspeakable,
Be merciful, *spare us, O Holy Trinity.*
Be merciful, *graciously hear us, O Holy Trinity.*
From all evil, *deliver us, O Holy Trinity.*
From all sin,**
From all pride,
From all love of riches,
From all uncleanness,
From all sloth,
From all inordinate affection,
From all envy and malice,
From all anger and impatience,
From every thought, word, and deed, contrary to Your holy law,
From Your everlasting malediction,
Through Your almighty power,
Through Your plenteous loving-kindness,
Through the exceeding treasures of Your goodness and love,

** *Deliver us, O Holy Trinity* is repeated after each invocation.

Through the depths of Your wisdom and knowledge,
Through all Your ineffable perfections,
We sinners,
*we beseech You, hear us.*
That we may ever serve You alone,***
That we may worship You in spirit and in truth,
That we may love You with all our heart, with all our soul, and with all our strength,
That, for Your sake, we may love our neighbor as ourselves,
That we may faithfully keep Your holy commandments,
That we may never defile our bodies and our souls with sin,
That we may go from grace to grace, and from virtue to virtue,
That we may finally enjoy the sight of You in glory,
That You would hear us,
O blessed Trinity,
*we beseech You, deliver us.*
O blessed Trinity,
*we beseech You, save us.*
O blessed Trinity,
*have mercy on us.*
Lord, have mercy.
*Christ, have mercy.*
Lord, have mercy.

℣. Blessed are you, O Lord, in the firmament of heaven.

℟. *And worthy to be praised, and glorious, and highly exalted forever.*

*** *We beseech you, hear us* is repeated after each invocation.

## Prayer in Praise of the Living Trinity

FATHER,
enable me to praise You,
and to sing to You,
my Lord and my Master,
through Whom are the ages without end,
the light of the sun and the beauty of the stars. . . .
You have created all things,
assigning to each a place,
and You govern them with Your Providence.
You spoke a word and Your work was accomplished.

Your Word is God the Son,
equal to You in substance and in dignity.
He rules over the world.

The Holy Spirit,
Who is God,
envelops all things
and watches over and protects them.

I proclaim that You are the living Trinity,
unique and sole Ruler;
immutable Nature, and without beginning;
ineffable Essence;
Intelligence Whose wisdom is inaccessible;
unshakable Power with no beginning or end;

Light Whom no one can see,
but Who see all things,
You are not ignorant of anything.
You know even the most profound things
from the earth to the netherworld.

Father, be gracious toward me.
Enable me to serve You in all Your majesty,

remove my sins far from me,
purify my conscience,
so that I may glorify Your Divinity
while lifting up toward Your pure hands,
so that I may bless Christ
and, bending the knee,
beg Him to accept me as His servant
when He comes as Judge in glory.

Father, be gracious toward me.
May I find mercy and grace.
For yours are the glory and praise
until the endless ages.

*Gregory Nazianzen*

## –6–

# Devotions to the Holy Spirit

## Prayer to Receive the Holy Spirit

O KING of glory,
send us the Promised of the Father,
the Spirit of Truth.
May the Counselor Who proceeds from You
enlighten us
and infuse all truth in us,
as You have promised.

## Prayer for the Seven Gifts of the Spirit

O LORD Jesus,
through You I humbly beg the merciful Father
to send the Holy Spirit of grace,
that He may bestow upon us His sevenfold gifts.

May He send us the gift of *wisdom,*
which will make us relish the Tree of Life
that is none other than Yourself;
the gift of *understanding,*
which will enlighten us;
the gift of *counsel,*
which will guide us in the way of righteousness;
and the gift of *fortitude,*
which will give us the strength to vanquish
the enemies of our sanctification and salvation.

May He impart to us the gift of *knowledge,*
which will enable us to discern Your teaching
and distinguish good from evil;
the gift of *piety,*
which will make us enjoy true peace;
and the gift of *fear,*
which will make us shun all iniquity
and avoid all danger of offending Your Majesty.
To the Father
and to the Son
and to the Holy Spirit
be given all glory and thanksgiving forever.

*St. Bonaventure*

## Prayer for the Twelve Fruits of the Spirit

HOLY Spirit,
eternal Love of the Father and the Son,
kindly bestow on us
the fruit of *charity,*
that we may be united to You by Divine love;
the fruit of *joy,*
that we may be filled with holy consolation;
the fruit of *peace,*
that we may enjoy tranquility of soul;

and the fruit of *patience,*
that we may endure humbly
everything that may be opposed to our own desires.

Divine Spirit,
be pleased to infuse in us
the fruit of *kindness,*
that we may willingly relieve our neighbor's necessities;
the fruit of *goodness,*
that we may be benevolent toward all;
the fruit of *patience,*
that we may not be discouraged by delay
but may persevere in prayer;
and the fruit of *mildness,*
that we may subdue every rising of ill temper,
stifle every murmur,
and repress the susceptibilities of our nature
in all our dealings with our neighbor.

Creator Spirit,
graciously impart to us
the fruit of *fidelity,*
that we may rely with assured confidence
on the word of God;
the fruit of *modesty,*
that we may order our exterior regularly;
and the fruits of *continence* and *chastity,*
that we may keep our bodies in such holiness
as befits Your temple,
so that having by Your assistance
preserved our hearts pure on earth,
we may merit in Jesus Christ,
according to the words of the Gospel,
to see God eternally
in the glory of His Kingdom.

## Prayer for Union with the Holy Spirit

O HOLY Spirit of Light and Love,
to You I consecrate my heart, mind, and will
for time and eternity.
May I be ever docile to Your Divine inspirations
and to the teachings of the holy Catholic Church
whose infallible guide You are.

May my heart be ever inflamed
with the love of God and love of neighbor.
May my will be ever in harmony with Your Divine Will.
May my life faithfully imitate the life and virtues
of our Lord and Savior Jesus Christ.
To Him,
with the Father,
and You, Divine Spirit,
be honor and glory forever.

*St. Pius X*

## Prayer for the Indwelling of the Spirit

HOLY Spirit,
powerful Consoler,
sacred Bond of the Father and the Son,
Hope of the afflicted,
descend into my heart
and establish in it Your loving dominion.
Enkindle in my tepid soul
the fire of Your Love
so that I may be wholly subject to You.

We believe that when You dwell in us,
You also prepare a dwelling
for the Father and the Son.
Deign, therefore, to come to me,

Consoler of abandoned souls,
and Protector of the needy.
Help the afflicted,
strengthen the weak,
and support the wavering.

Come and purify me.
Let no evil desire take possession of me.
You love the humble and resist the proud.
Come to me,
Glory of the living,
and Hope of the dying.
Lead me by Your grace
that I may always be pleasing to You.

*St. Augustine of Hippo*

## Prayer to the Holy Spirit for Unbelievers

HOLY Spirit,
on the first Pentecost,
through Your inspiration many were transformed,
becoming adopted children of God
and faithful disciples of Jesus Christ.
They were animated by the love of God
that is poured into us
by You, Holy Spirit,
Who are given to us.

Enlighten the minds of unbelievers,
incline their wills to accept the Good News,
and prompt them to be obedient
to the Teachers of the Church
about whom Christ said:
"Whoever listens to you listens to Me,
and whoever rejects you rejects Me" (Luke 10:16).
Teach them how to pray

and prepare their minds and hearts
for Your coming into their souls.

## Litany of the Holy Spirit

LORD, have mercy.
*Christ, have mercy.*
Lord, have mercy. Holy Spirit, hear us.
*Holy Spirit, graciously hear us.*
God, the Father of heaven, *have mercy on us.*
God, the Son, Redeemer of the world, *
God, the Holy Spirit,
Holy Trinity, one God,
Holy Spirit, Who proceed from the Father and the Son,
Holy Spirit, co-equal with the Father and the Son,
Promise of the Father, most bounteous,
Gift of God most high,
Ray of heavenly Light,
Author of all good,
Source of living Water,
Consuming Fire,
Burning Love,
Spiritual Unction,
Spirit of truth and power,
Spirit of wisdom and understanding,
Spirit of counsel and fortitude,
Spirit of knowledge and piety,
Spirit of fear of the Lord,
Spirit of penitence,
Spirit of grace and prayer,
Spirit of charity, peace, and joy,
Spirit of patience,
Spirit of goodness,
Spirit of kindness and mildness,

* *Have mercy on us* is repeated after each invocation.

Spirit of fidelity,
Spirit of modesty and continence,
Spirit of chastity,
Spirit of adoption of children of God,
Holy Spirit, comforter,
Holy Spirit, sanctifier,
You through Whom spoke holy men of God,
You Who overshadowed Mary,
You by Whom Mary conceived Christ,
You Who descend upon human beings at Baptism,
You Who, on the Day of Pentecost, appeared through fiery tongues,
You by Whom we are reborn,
You Who dwell in us as in a temple,
You Who govern and animate the Church,
You Who fill the whole world,
That You may renew the face of the earth,
*we beseech You, hear us.*
That You may shed Your Light upon us, **
That You may pour Your Love into our hearts,
That You may inspire us to love our neighbor,
That You may teach us to ask for the graces we need,
That You may enlighten us with Your heavenly inspirations,
That You may guide us in the way of holiness,
That You may make us obedient to Your commandments,
That You may teach us how to pray,
That You may always pray with us,
That You may inspire us with horror for sin,
That You may direct us in the practice of virtue,

** *We beseech You, hear us* is repeated after each invocation.

That You may make us persevere in a holy life,
That You may make us faithful to our vocation,
That You may grant us good priests and Bishops,
That You may give us good Christian families,
That You may grant us a spiritual renewal of the Church,
That You may guide and console the Holy Father,
Lamb of God, You take away the sins of the world; *spare us, O Lord.*
Lamb of God, You take away the sins of the world; *graciously hear us, O Lord.*
Lamb of God, You take away the sins of the world; *have mercy on us.*
Holy Spirit, hear us.
*Holy Spirit, graciously hear us.*
Lord, have mercy.
*Christ, have mercy.*
Lord, have mercy.
℣. Create a clean heart in us.
℟. *Renew a right spirit in us.*

Let us pray.
O merciful Father,
grant that Your Divine Spirit
may cleanse, inflame, and enlighten our minds and hearts.
Enable us to be fruitful in good works
for the glory of Your Majesty
and the spiritual and material well-being of all people.
We ask this through Jesus Christ Your Son
and the Holy Spirit.

–7–

# Devotions to the Blessed Virgin Mary

## The Holy Rosary

RELIGIOUS devotion, public or private, for the duration of nine days to gain special graces, is called a Novena. Those who perform it with a lively hope of having their request granted, and with perfect resignation should it be refused, may be assured that Christ will grant some grace or blessing, though in His infinite wisdom and mercy He may refuse the particular favor which they implore.

Novenas originated in imitation of the Apostles who were gathered together in prayer for nine days from the time of Our Lord's Ascension to Pentecost Sunday. However, care must be taken lest the power of any Novena be limited to the number *nine* rather than perseverance in fervent prayer.

The practice of saying the Rosary nine times in the form of a Rosary Novena in *petition* or *thanksgiving* is another way of heeding Our Lady of Fatima's admonition to *Pray the Rosary.*

The 54-Day Novena Devotion, which originated in 1884 at the Sanctuary of Our Lady of the Rosary of Pompei, consists of the daily recitation of five decades of the Rosary for twenty-seven days in *petition* and five decades for twenty-seven additional days in *thanksgiving.* In reality you will be making three Novenas *in petition* for *a particular favor* and three Novenas in *thanksgiving* for a *particular favor.*

1st day say the 5 Joyful Mysteries.

2nd day say the 5 Sorrowful Mysteries.

3rd day say the 5 Glorious Mysteries.

4th day begin again the 5 Joyful Mysteries, etc.*

## The Family Rosary

### The Family That Prays Together . . . Stays Together

THE Family Rosary is the Rosary recited *aloud together,* by as many of the family and their friends as can be present, or even by only two. Any family may say the Family Rosary in any suitable place and at any time.

A leader says aloud the first part of each prayer; a second person or group of persons answers aloud the second part of that prayer.

To begin the Family Rosary, all hold the Crucifix of their Rosary in the right hand and make the Sign of the Cross.

The leader begins the Apostles' Creed and proceeds to say the Our Father on the large beads and the Hail Mary on the small beads. The leader announces the Mystery before each decade. Five decades should be recited each day.

* *Note:* the Mysteries of Light recommended by Pope John Paul II could be inserted in this Novena on the 2nd day, dropping the Sorrowful and the Glorious Mysteries each one day (to the 3rd and 4th days, respectively). The Joyful Mysteries could begin again on the 5th day.

## The Five First Saturdays

### Mary's Great Promise at Fatima

THE Five First Saturdays are intended to honor and to make reparation to the Immaculate Heart of Mary for all the blasphemies and ingratitude of people.

This devotion and the wonderful promises connected with it were revealed by the Blessed Virgin at Fatima, a small village in Portugal. Our Lady appeared to three children there in 1917, and one of the little girls, Lucy, tells us that she said: *I promise to help at the hour of death, with the graces needed for salvation, whoever on the First Saturday of five consecutive months shall:*

1. *Confess and receive Communion;*

2. *Recite five decades of the Rosary;*

3. *And keep me company for fifteen minutes while meditating on the fifteen Mysteries of the Rosary, with the intention of making reparation to me.*

## Prayer before the Rosary

QUEEN of the Holy Rosary, you have deigned to come to Fatima to reveal to the three shepherd children the treasures of grace hidden in the Rosary. Inspire my heart with a sincere love of this devotion, in order that by meditating on the Mysteries of our Redemption which are recalled in it, I may be enriched with its fruits and obtain peace for the world, the conversion of sinners, and the favor which I ask of you in this Rosary. *(Here mention your request.)* I ask it for the greater glory of God, for your own honor, and for the good of souls, especially for my own. Amen.

## The Five Joyful Mysteries

*(Said on Mondays and Saturdays, and Sundays from Advent until Lent)*

*The Joyful Mysteries direct our mind to the Son of God, Jesus Christ, our Lord and Savior, Who took human nature from a human mother, Mary. They also bring to our attention some of the extraordinary events that preceded, accompanied, and followed Christ's birth.*

### 1. The Annunciation

Lk 1:26-38; Isa 7:10-15

MARY, you received with deep humility the news of the Angel Gabriel that you were to be the Mother of God's Son; obtain for me a similar *humility.*

### 2. The Visitation

Lk 1:39-56

MARY, you showed true charity in visiting Elizabeth and remaining with her for three months before the birth of John the Baptist; obtain for me the grace to *love my neighbor.*

### 3. The Birth of Jesus

Lk 2:1-14; Mt 1:18-24; Gal 4:1-7

JESUS, You lovingly accepted poverty when You were placed in the manger in the stable although You were our God and Redeemer; grant that I may have the *spirit of poverty.*

### 4. The Presentation in the Temple
Lk 2:22-38

MARY, you obeyed the law of God in presenting the Child Jesus in the Temple; obtain for me the *virtue of obedience.*

### 5. The Finding in the Temple
Lk 2:42-50

MARY, you were filled with sorrow at the loss of Jesus and overwhelmed with joy on finding Him surrounded by Teachers in the Temple; obtain for me the *virtue of piety.*

## The Five Luminous Mysteries*

*(Said on Thursdays [except during Lent])*

*The Luminous Mysteries recall to our mind important events of the Public Ministry of Christ through which He announces the coming of the Kingdom of God, bears witness to it in His works, and proclaims its demands—showing that the Mystery of Christ is most evidently a Mystery of Light.*

### 1. Christ's Baptism in the Jordan

Mt 3:13-17; Isa 42:1-2, 4-5

**JESUS, at Your Baptism in the Jordan, the Father called You His beloved Son and the Holy Spirit descended upon You to invest You with Your mission; help me to keep my *Baptismal Promises.***

### 2. Christ's Self-Manifestation at the Wedding in Cana

Jn 2:1-11

**MARY, the first among believers in Christ, as a result of your intercession at Cana, your Son changed water into wine and opened the hearts of the disciples to faith; obtain for me the grace to *do whatever Jesus says.***

* Added to the Mysteries of the Rosary by Pope John Paul II in his Apostolic Letter of October 16, 2002, entitled *The Rosary of the Virgin Mary*. They are reprinted here from our book *Pray the Rosary*, which in 2002 received the Imprimatur from Most Rev. Frank J. Rodimer, Bishop of Paterson.

### 3. Christ's Proclamation of the Kingdom of God
Mk 1:14-15; Mt 5:1-11

JESUS, You preached the Kingdom of God with its call to forgiveness, inaugurating the ministry of mercy, which You continue to exercise, especially through the Sacrament of Reconciliation; help me to *seek forgiveness for my sins.*

### 4. The Transfiguration of Our Lord
Mt 17:1-8; Mk 9:2-8; Lk 9:28-36

JESUS, at Your Transfiguration, the glory of the Godhead shone forth from Your face as the Father commanded the Apostles to hear You and be transfigured by the Holy Spirit; help me to *be a new person in You.*

### 5. Christ's Institution of the Eucharist
Mt 26:26-28; 1 Cor 11:23-25

JESUS, at the Last Supper, You instituted the Eucharist, offering Your Body and Blood as food under the signs of bread and wine and testifying to Your love for humanity; help me to *attain active participation at Mass.*

## The Five Sorrowful Mysteries

*(Said on Tuesdays and Fridays throughout the year, and daily from Ash Wednesday until Easter Sunday)*

*The Sorrowful Mysteries recall to our mind the mysterious events surrounding Christ's sacrifice of His life in order that sinful humanity might be reconciled with God.*

### 1. The Agony in the Garden
Mt 26:36-46

JESUS, in the Garden of Gethsemane, You suffered a bitter agony because of our sins; grant me *true contrition.*

### 2. The Scourging at the Pillar
Mt 27:26

JESUS, You endured a cruel scourging and Your flesh was torn by heavy blows; help me to have the *virtue of purity.*

### 3. The Crowning with Thorns
Mt 27:27-31

JESUS, You patiently endured the pain from the crown of sharp thorns that was forced upon Your head; grant me the strength to have *moral courage.*

### 4. The Carrying of the Cross

Mt 27:32

JESUS, You willingly carried Your Cross for love of Your Father and all people; grant me the *virtue of patience.*

### 5. The Crucifixion

Mt 27:33-50; Jn 19:17-30

JESUS, for love of me You endured hours of torture on the Cross and gave up Your spirit; grant me the grace of *final perseverance.*

## The Five Glorious Mysteries

*(Said on Wednesdays [except during Lent] and the Sundays from Easter until Advent)*

*The Glorious Mysteries recall to our mind the ratification of Christ's sacrifice for the redemption of the world, and our sharing in the fruits of His sacrifice.*

### 1. The Resurrection

Mk 16:1-7; Jn 20:1-10

JESUS, You rose from the dead in triumph and remained for forty days with Your disciples, instructing and encouraging them; increase my *faith.*

### 2. The Ascension

Mk 16:19-20; Acts 1:9-11

JESUS, in the presence of Mary and the disciples You ascended to heaven to sit at the Father's right hand; increase the *virtue of hope* in me.

### 3. The Descent of the Holy Spirit

Jn 14:15-31; Acts 2:1-11

JESUS, in fulfillment of Your promise You sent the Holy Spirit upon Mary and the disciples under the form of tongues of fire; increase my *love for God.*

### 4. The Assumption

Lk 1:41-50; Ps 45; Gen 3:15

MARY, by the power of God you were assumed into heaven and united with your Divine Son; help me to have *true devotion to you.*

### 5. The Crowning of the Blessed Virgin

Rev 12:1; Jud 13:18-20; 15:9-10

MARY, you were crowned Queen of heaven by Your Divine Son to the great joy of all the Saints; obtain *eternal happiness* for me.

*At the end of the Rosary, one may add the prayer "The Hail! Holy Queen" and the Prayer after the Rosary. Both* *can be found on p. 223.*

## The Prayers of the Rosary

### The Our Father

OUR Father, Who art in heaven, hallowed be Thy name; Thy kingdom come, Thy will be done on earth as it is in heaven. Give us this day our daily bread, and forgive us our trespasses, as we forgive those who trespass against us; and lead us not into temptation, but deliver us from evil. Amen.

### The Hail Mary

HAIL Mary, full of grace, the Lord is with you; blessed are you among women, and blessed is the fruit of your womb, Jesus. Holy Mary, Mother of God, pray for us sinners now and at the hour of our death. Amen.

### Glory Be to the Father

GLORY be to the Father, and to the Son, and to the Holy Spirit. As it was in the beginning, is now, and ever shall be, world without end. Amen.

### The Apostles' Creed

I BELIEVE in God, the Father Almighty, Creator of heaven and earth, and in Jesus Christ, His only Son, our Lord, who was conceived by the Holy Spirit, born of the Virgin Mary, suffered under Pontius Pilate, was crucified, died and was buried; he descended into hell; on the third day He rose again from the dead; He ascended into heaven, and is seated at the right hand of God, the Father Almighty; from there He will come to judge the living and the dead. I believe in the Holy Spirit, the holy catholic Church, the communion of saints, the forgiveness of sins, the resurrection of the body, and life everlasting. Amen.

## The Hail! Holy Queen

HAIL! Holy Queen, Mother of Mercy, our life, our sweetness, and our hope. To you do we cry, poor banished children of Eve. To you do we send up our sighs, mourning and weeping in this valley of tears. Turn then, O most gracious advocate, your eyes of mercy toward us; and after this our exile, show unto us the blessed fruit of your womb, Jesus. O clement! O loving! O sweet Virgin Mary!

℣. Pray for us, O Holy Mother of God.

℟. *That we may be made worthy of the promises of Christ.*

## Prayer after the Rosary

O GOD, Whose only-begotten Son, by His Life, Death, and Resurrection, has purchased for us the rewards of eternal life; grant, we beseech You, that, meditating upon these Mysteries of the Most Holy Rosary of the Blessed Virgin Mary, we may imitate what they contain and obtain what they promise, through the same Christ our Lord. Amen.

℣. May the divine assistance remain always with us.

℟. *Amen.*

℣. And may the souls of the faithful departed, through the mercy of God, rest in peace.

℟. *Amen.*

## MIRACULOUS MEDAL NOVENA

### Opening Prayer

COME, Holy Spirit, fill the hearts of Your faithful, and kindle in them the fire of Your love. Send forth Your Spirit, and they shall be created; and You shall renew the face of the earth.

O God, You instructed the hearts of the faithful by the light of the Holy Spirit. Grant us in the same Spirit to be truly wise and ever to rejoice in His consolation, through Jesus Christ our Lord. Amen.

O Mary, conceived without sin, pray for us who have recourse to you. *(3 times.)*

Lord Jesus Christ, You have been pleased to glorify by numberless miracles the Blessed Virgin Mary, immaculate from the first moment of her conception. Grant that all who devoutly implore her protection on earth may eternally enjoy Your presence in heaven, Who, with the Father and the Holy Spirit, live and reign, God, forever and ever. Amen.

Lord Jesus Christ, for the accomplishment of Your works, You have chosen the weak things of the world, that no flesh may glory in Your sight. And for a better and more widely diffused belief in the Immaculate Conception of Your Mother, You have wished that the Miraculous Medal be manifested to Saint Catherine Labouré. Grant, we beseech You, that filled with like humility, we may glorify this mystery by word and work. Amen.

## Memorare

REMEMBER, O most gracious Virgin Mary, that never was it known that anyone who fled to your protection, implored your help, or sought your intercession, was left unaided. Inspired with this confidence, I fly to you, O Virgin of virgins, my Mother. To you I come, before you I stand, sinful and sorrowful. O Mother of the Word Incarnate, despise not my petitions, but in your mercy hear and answer me. Amen.

### NOVENA PRAYER

IMMACULATE Virgin Mary, Mother of our Lord Jesus Christ and our Mother, penetrated with the most lively confidence in your all-powerful and never-failing intercession, manifested so often through the Miraculous Medal, we your loving and trustful children implore you to obtain for us the graces and favors we ask during this Novena, if they be beneficial to our immortal souls, and the souls for which we pray. *(Here mention your request.)*

You know, Mary, how often our souls have been the sanctuaries of your Son Who hates iniquity. Obtain for us then a deep hatred of sin and that purity of heart which will attach us to God alone so that our every thought, word, and deed may tend to His greater glory.

Obtain for us also a spirit of prayer and self-denial that we may recover by penance what we have lost by sin and at length attain to that blessed abode where you are the Queen of Angels and of People. Amen.

## Act of Consecration

VIRGIN Mother of God, Mary Immaculate, we dedicate and consecrate ourselves to you under the title of Our Lady of the Miraculous Medal. May this Medal be a sure sign of your affection for us and a constant reminder of our duties toward you. Ever while wearing it, may we be blessed by your loving protection and preserved in the grace of your Son.

Most powerful Virgin, Mother of our Savior, keep us close to you every moment of our lives. Obtain for us, your children, the grace of a happy death; so that, in union with you, we may enjoy the blessing of heaven forever. Amen.

Mary, conceived without sin, pray for us who have recourse to you. *(3 times.)*

## Litany of the Blessed Virgin Mary

LORD, have mercy.
*Christ, have mercy.*
Lord, have mercy.
Christ, hear us.
*Christ, graciously hear us.*
God, the Father of heaven, *have mercy on us.*
God the Son, Redeemer of the world,
*have mercy on us.*
God the Holy Spirit,
*have mercy on us.*
Holy Trinity, one God, *have mercy on us.*
Holy Mary, *pray for us.* *
Holy Mother of God,
Holy Virgin of virgins,
Mother of Christ,

* *Pray for us* is repeated after each invocation.

Mother of the Church,
Mother of mercy,
Mother of Divine grace,
Mother of hope,
Mother most pure,
Mother most chaste,
Mother inviolate,
Mother undefiled,
Mother most amiable,
Mother most admirable,
Mother of good counsel,
Mother of our Creator,
Mother of our Savior,
Virgin most prudent,
Virgin most venerable,
Virgin most renowned,
Virgin most powerful,
Virgin most merciful,
Virgin most faithful,
Mirror of justice,
Seat of wisdom,
Cause of our joy,
Spiritual vessel,
Vessel of honor,
Singular vessel of devotion,
Mystical rose,
Tower of David,
Tower of ivory,
House of gold,
Ark of the covenant,
Gate of heaven,
Morning star,
Health of the sick,
Refuge of sinners,
Solace of migrants,

Comforter of the afflicted,
Help of Christians,
Queen of Angels,
Queen of Patriarchs,
Queen of Prophets,
Queen of Apostles,
Queen of Martyrs,
Queen of Confessors,
Queen of Virgins,
Queen of all Saints,
Queen conceived without original sin,
Queen assumed into heaven,
Queen of the most holy Rosary,
Queen of families,
Queen of peace,

Lamb of God, You take away the sins of the world; *spare us, O Lord!*
Lamb of God, You take away the sins of the world; *graciously hear us, O Lord!*
Lamb of God, You take away the sins of the world; *have mercy on us.*
℣. Pray for us, O holy Mother of God.
℟. *That we may be made worthy of the promises of Christ.*

Let us pray.
Grant, we beg You, O Lord God,
that we Your servants
may enjoy lasting health of mind and body,
and by the glorious intercession
of the Blessed Mary, ever Virgin,
be delivered from present sorrow
and enter into the joy of eternal happiness.
Through Christ our Lord.
℟. *Amen.*

## During Advent

Let us pray.
O God,
You willed that, at the message of an Angel,
Your Word should take flesh
in the womb of the Blessed Virgin Mary;
grant to Your suppliant people,
that we, who believe her to be truly the Mother of God,
may be helped by her intercession with You.
Through the same Christ our Lord.
℟. *Amen.*

## From Christmas to the Purification

Let us pray.
O God,
by the fruitful virginity of Blessed Mary,
You bestowed upon the human race
the rewards of eternal salvation;
grant, we beg You,
that we may feel the power of her intercession,
through whom we have been made worthy
to receive the Author of life,
our Lord Jesus Christ Your Son,
Who lives and reigns with You forever and ever.
℟. *Amen.*

## During Easter Time

Let us pray.
O God,
Who by the Resurrection of Your Son,
our Lord Jesus Christ,
granted joy to the whole world,

grant, we beg you,
that through the intercession of the Virgin Mary,
His Mother,
we may attain the joys of eternal life.
Through the same Christ our Lord.
℟. *Amen.*

*—8—*

# Devotions to Saint Joseph

## Novena to Saint Joseph

### Invocation

THE just man will blossom like the palm tree—
and flourish forever before the Lord.

### Reading

Whatever you do, do it wholeheartedly, as if you were doing it for the Lord and not for others,
since you know that you will receive from the Lord
an inheritance as your reward for you are serving the Lord Christ. *Colossians 3:23-24*

### Prayer to Saint Joseph

O BLESSED Saint Joseph,
loving father and faithful guardian of Jesus, and
devoted spouse of the Mother of God,
I beg you to offer God the Father
His Divine Son, bathed in blood on the Cross.

Through the holy Name of Jesus
obtain for us from the Father
the favor we implore.

Appease the Divine anger so justly inflamed by our crimes;
beg of Jesus love for your children.
Amid the splendors of eternity,
forget not the sorrows of those who suffer,
those who pray and those who weep.
Stay the almighty arm that smites us
so that by your prayers and those of your Spouse
the Heart of Jesus may be moved to pity and pardon.

## Concluding Prayer

HEAVENLY Father,
You entrusted to the faithful care of Joseph
the beginnings of the mysteries of our salvation.
Through his intercession
may Your Church always be faithful in her service
so that Your designs may be fulfilled.
We ask this through Christ our Lord.

## Litany of Saint Joseph

LORD, have mercy.
*Christ, have mercy.*
Lord, have mercy.
Christ, hear us.
*Christ, graciously hear us.*
God, the Father of Heaven, *have mercy on us.*
God the Son, Redeemer of the world,
*have mercy on us.*

God the Holy Spirit,
*have mercy on us.*
Holy Trinity, one God,
*have mercy on us.*
Holy Mary, *pray for us.* *
Saint Joseph,
Renowned offspring of David,
Light of Patriarchs,
Spouse of the Mother of God,
Guardian of the Redeemer,
Chaste guardian of the Virgin,
Foster father of the Son of God,
Diligent protector of Christ,
Servant of Christ,
Minister of salvation,
Head of the Holy Family,
Joseph most just,
Joseph most chaste,
Joseph most prudent,
Joseph most strong,
Joseph most obedient,
Joseph most faithful,
Mirror of patience,
Lover of poverty,
Model of artisans,
Glory of home life,
Guardian of Virgins,
Pillar of families,
Support in difficulties,
Solace of the wretched,
Hope of the sick,
Patron of exiles,
Patron of the afflicted,

* *Pray for us* is repeated after each invocation.

Patron of the poor,
Patron of the dying,
Terror of demons,
Protector of Holy Church,
Lamb of God, You take away the sins of the world; *spare us, O Lord!*
Lamb of God, You take away the sins of the world; *graciously hear us, O Lord!*
Lamb of God, You take away the sins of the world; *have mercy on us.*
℣. He made him the lord of His household.
℟. *And prince over all His possessions.*

Let us pray.
O God,
in Your ineffable Providence
You were pleased to choose Blessed Joseph
to be the spouse of Your most holy Mother;
grant, we beg You,
that we may be worthy
to have him for our intercessor in heaven
whom on earth we venerate as our Protector:
You Who live and reign forever and ever.
℟. *Amen.*

**–9–**

# Devotions to the Infant Jesus

## The Holy Infancy

ADORABLE Child Jesus,
in You
wisdom resides,
Divinity dwells,
and all eternal riches are found.

You are the beauty of heaven,
the delight of the Angels,
and the salvation of humankind.
Here I am prostrated at Your feet,
O Source of innocence, purity, and holiness.
Although I am a slave of sin,
I belong to You by the undeniable right
of Your sovereignty.

I hereby render to You as my Lord—
my King and my dignified and most adorable Savior—
my faith and my homage with the shepherds,
and my act of adoration with the Magi.
I give myself entirely and without restriction
into Your powerful hands,
which drew all the universe from nothingness
and preserved it in the admirable order
that we see.

O lovable Child,
grant that as a result of my total devotion
to honoring the mystery of Your Divine Childhood,
I may have the happiness—
through the mediation of Your holy Mother
and St. Joseph, Your foster father—
to live all the rest of my life
in the same manner as You.
May I live in You,
for You,
and under the direction of Your Divine Spirit,
so that not one moment of my life
deviates from Your Will,
or forestalls it in any respect,

but listens to it
and faithfully follows it in every way.

## Litany to the Infant Jesus

(For Private Devotion)

LORD, have mercy.
*Christ, have mercy.*
Lord, have mercy.
Jesus, hear us.
*Jesus, graciously hear us.*
God the Father of heaven, *have mercy on us.*
God, the Son, Redeemer of the world,*
God, the Holy Spirit,
Holy Trinity, one God,
Infant, Jesus Christ,
Infant, true God,
Infant, Son of the living God,
Infant, Son of the Virgin Mary,
Infant, strong in weakness,
Infant, powerful in tenderness,
Infant, treasure of grace,
Infant, fountain of love,
Infant, renewer of the heavens,
Infant, repairer of the evils of earth,
Infant, head of the Angels,
Infant, root of the Patriarchs
Infant, speech of Prophets,
Infant, desire of the Gentiles,
Infant, joy of Shepherds,
Infant, light of the Magi,
Infant, salvation of Infants,
Infant, expectation of the just,
Infant, instructor of the wise,

* *Have mercy on us* is repeated after each invocation.

Infant, firstfruits of all Saints,
Be merciful, *spare us, O Infant Jesus.*
Be merciful, *graciously hear us, O Infant Jesus.*
From the slavery of the children of Adam, *Infant Jesus, deliver us.*
From the slavery of the devil,**
From the evil desires of the flesh,
From the malice of the world,
From the pride of life,
From the inordinate desire of knowing,
From the blindness of spirit,
From an evil will,
From our sins,
Through Your most pure Conception,
Through Your most humble Nativity,
Through Your tears,
Through Your most painful Circumcision,
Through Your most glorious Epiphany,
Through Your most pious Presentation,
Through Your most Divine life,
Through Your poverty,
Through Your many sufferings,
Through Your labors and travels,
Lamb of God, You take away the sins of the world; *have mercy on us, O Infant Jesus.*
Lamb of God, You take away the sins of the world; *graciously hear us, O Infant Jesus.*
Lamb of God, You take away the sins of the world; *have mercy on us.*
℣. Jesus, Infant, hear us.
℟. *Jesus, Infant, graciously hear us.*

** *Infant Jesus, deliver us* is repeated after each invocation.

### Prayer to the Infant Jesus

LET us pray.
O Lord Christ,
You were pleased so to humble Yourself
in Your incarnate Divinity
and most sacred Humanity,
as to be born in time
and become a little Child.

Grant that we may acknowledge
infinite wisdom in the silence of a Child,
power in weakness,
and majesty in humiliation.

Adoring Your humiliations on earth,
may we contemplate Your glories in heaven,
Who with the Father and the Holy Spirit
live and reign forever.

*–10–*

## Devotions to the Angels

### Prayer to Saint Michael

SAINT Michael the Archangel, defend us in battle, be our protection against the wickedness and snares of the devil; may God rebuke him, we humbly pray; and do you, O Prince of the heavenly host, by the power of God, thrust into hell Satan and all evil spirits who wander through the world for the ruin of souls. Amen.

Saint Michael the Archangel, defend us in the battle, that we may not perish in the fearful judgment.

Saint Michael, first champion of the Kingship of Christ, pray for us.

God our Father, in a wonderful way You guide the work of Angels and human beings. May those who serve You constantly in heaven keep our lives safe from all harm on earth. Grant this through Christ our Lord. Amen.

## Litany in Honor of Saint Michael

(For Private Devotion)

LORD, have mercy.
*Christ, have mercy.*
Lord, have mercy.
Christ, hear us.
*Christ, graciously hear us.*
God the Father of heaven, *have mercy on us.*
God the Son, Redeemer of the world,
God the Holy Spirit,
Holy Trinity, one God,
Holy Mary, Queen of the Angels, *pray for us.*
Saint Michael, the Archangel,*
Most glorious attendant of the Triune Divinity,
Standing at the right of the altar of incense,
Ambassador of Paradise,
Glorious Prince of the heavenly armies,
Leader of the angelic hosts,
The standard-bearer of God's armies,
Defender of Divine glory,
First defender of the Kingship of Christ,
Strength of God,
Invincible prince and warrior,
Angel of Peace,
Guide of Christ,

* *Pray for us* is repeated after each invocation.

Guardian of the Christian Faith,
Champion of God's people,
Guardian Angel of the Eucharist,
Defender of the Church,
Protector of the Sovereign Pontiff,
Angel of Catholic apostolic work,
Powerful intercessor of Christians,
Brave defender of those who hope in God,
Guardian of our souls and bodies,
Healer of the sick,
Help of those in their agony,
Consoler of the souls in purgatory,
God's messenger for the souls of the just,
Terror of the evil spirits,
Victorious in battle against evil,
Guardian and Patron of the universal Church,
Lamb of God, You take away the sins of the world; *spare us, O Lord.*
Lamb of God, You take away the sins of the world; *graciously hear us, O Lord.*
Lamb of God, You take away the sins of the world; *have mercy on us.*
℣. Pray for us, O glorious Saint Michael,
℟. *That we may be made worthy of the promises of Christ.*

Let us pray. Relying, Lord, upon the intercession of Your blessed Archangel Michael, we humbly beg of You, that the Sacrament of the Eucharist that we have received may make our souls holy and pleasing to You. We ask this through Christ our Lord.
℟. *Amen.*

## Prayer to Saint Gabriel

SAINT Gabriel the Archangel, I venerate you as the "Angel of the Incarnation," because God has specially appointed you to bear the messages concerning the God-Man to Daniel, Zechariah, and the Blessed Virgin Mary. Give me a very tender and devoted love for the Incarnate Word and His blessed Mother, more like your own.

I venerate you also as the "strength from God," because you are the giver of God's strength, consoler and comforter chosen to strengthen God's faithful and to teach them important truths. I ask for the grace of a special power of the will to strive for holiness of life. Steady my resolutions, renew my courage, comfort and console me in the problems, trials, and sufferings of daily living, as you consoled our Savior in His agony and Mary in her sorrows and Joseph in his trials. I put my confidence in you.

Saint Gabriel, I ask you especially for this favor. *(Here mention your request.)* Through your earnest love for the Son of God-Made-Man and for His blessed Mother, I beg of you, intercede for me that my request may be granted, if it be God's holy Will.

℣. Pray for us, Saint Gabriel the Archangel.
℟. *That we may be made worthy of the promises of Christ.*

Let us pray. Almighty and ever-living God, since You chose the Archangel Gabriel from among all the Angels to announce the mystery of Your Son's Incarnation, mercifully grant that we who honor

him on earth may feel the benefit of his patronage in heaven. You live and reign forever.
℟. *Amen.*

## Litany in Honor of Saint Gabriel

(For Private Devotion)

LORD, have mercy
*Christ, have mercy.*
Lord, have mercy.
Christ, hear us.
*Christ, graciously hear us.*
God the Father of heaven, *have mercy on us.*
God the Son, Redeemer of the world,
God the Holy Spirit,
Holy Trinity, one God,
Jesus, King of Angels,
Mary, Queen of Angels, *pray for us.*
Saint Gabriel the Archangel,*
Strength from God,
Teacher of the nations,
Angel of the Incarnation,
Messenger of God's revelation,
Bearer of the "good news" of Redemption,
Faithful ambassador of God to Zechariah and the Virgin Mary,
Faithful Servant of the God-Man,
Angel of consolation at the Savior's agony,
Friend and consoler of the Mother of God,
Guide and helper of Saint Joseph,
Teacher and support of the prophet Daniel,
Patron of parents and teachers,
Guide to union with Jesus and Mary,
Consoler of those who suffer,

* *Pray for us* is repeated after each invocation.

Strength of the weak,
Patron saint of modern communications,
Lamb of God, You take away the sins of the world; *spare us, O Lord.*
Lamb of God, You take away the sins of the world; *graciously hear us, O Lord.*
Lamb of God, You take away the sins of the world; *have mercy on us.*

℣. Pray for us, Saint Gabriel the Archangel.
℟. *That we may be made worthy of the promises of Christ.*

Let us pray. O God, with great wisdom You direct the ministry of Angels and human beings. Grant that those who always minister to You in heaven may defend us during our life on earth. We ask this through Christ our Lord.
℟. *Amen.*

## Prayer to Saint Raphael

HOLY Archangel Raphael, standing so close to the throne of God and offering Him our prayers, I venerate you as God's special Friend and Messenger. I choose you as my Patron and wish to love and obey you as young Tobiah did. I consecrate to you my body and soul, all my work, and my whole life. I want you to be my Guide and Counselor in all the dangerous and difficult problems and decisions of my life.

Remember, dearest Saint Raphael, that the grace of God preserved you with the good Angels in heaven when the proud ones were cast into hell. I entreat you, therefore, to help me in my struggle against the world, the spirit of impurity, and the devil. Defend me from all dangers and every occasion of sin. Direct me always in the way of peace, safety, and salvation. Offer my prayers to God as you offered those of Tobiah, so that through your intercession I may obtain the graces necessary for the salvation of my soul. I ask you to pray that God grant me this favor if it be His holy Will. *(Here mention your request.)*

Saint Raphael, help me to love and serve my God faithfully, to die in His grace, and finally to merit to join you in seeing and praising God forever in heaven. Amen.

## Litany in Honor of Saint Raphael

(For Private Devotion)

LORD, have mercy.
*Christ, have mercy.*
Lord, have mercy.
Christ hear us.
*Christ, graciously hear us.*
God the Father of heaven, *have mercy on us.*
God the Son, Redeemer of the world,
God the Holy Spirit,
Holy Trinity, one God,
Jesus, King of Angels,
Mary, Queen of Angels, *pray for us.*
Saint Raphael the Archangel,*
Saint Raphael, whose name means "God has healed,"
Saint Raphael, preserved with the good Angels in God's Kingdom,
Saint Raphael, one of the seven spirits who stand before the Most High,

* *Pray for us* is repeated after each invocation.

Saint Raphael, ministering to God in heaven,
Saint Raphael, noble and mighty Messenger of God,
Saint Raphael, devoted to the Holy Will of God,
Saint Raphael, who offered to God the prayers of the father Tobit,
Saint Raphael, traveling companion of the young Tobiah,
Saint Raphael, who guarded your friends from danger,
Saint Raphael, who found a worthy wife for Tobiah,
Saint Raphael, who delivered Sarah from the evil spirits,
Saint Raphael, who healed the father Tobit of his blindness,
Saint Raphael, guide and protector on our journey through life,
Saint Raphael, strong helper in time of need,
Saint Raphael, conqueror of evil,
Saint Raphael, guide and counselor of your people,
Saint Raphael, protector of pure souls,
Saint Raphael, patron Angel of youth,
Saint Raphael, Angel of joy,
Saint Raphael, Angel of happy meetings,
Saint Raphael, Angel of chaste courtship,
Saint Raphael, Angel of those seeking a marriage partner,
Saint Raphael, Angel of a happy marriage,
Saint Raphael, Angel of home life,
Saint Raphael, Guardian of the Christian family,
Saint Raphael, protector of travelers,
Saint Raphael, patron of health,

Saint Raphael, heavenly physician,
Saint Raphael, helper of the blind,
Saint Raphael, healer of the sick,
Saint Raphael, patron of physicians,
Saint Raphael, consoler of the afflicted,
Saint Raphael, support of the dying,
Saint Raphael, herald of blessings,
Saint Raphael, defender of the Church,
Lamb of God, You take away the sins of the world; *spare us, O Lord.*
Lamb of God, You take away the sins of the world; *graciously hear us, O Lord.*
Lamb of God, You take away the sins of the world; *have mercy on us.*
℣. Pray for us, O glorious Saint Raphael the Archangel,
℟. *That we may be made worthy of the promises of Christ.*

Let us pray. God, You graciously gave the Archangel Raphael as a companion to Your servant Tobiah on his journey. Grant us, Your servants, that we may ever enjoy his protection and be strengthened by his help. We ask this through Christ our Lord.

℟. *Amen.*

## Prayer to Our Guardian Angel

O MOST faithful companion,
appointed by God to be my guardian,
and who never leave my side,
how shall I thank you for your faithfulness and love
and for the benefits that you have obtained for me!
You watch over me when I sleep;

you comfort me when I am sad;
you avert the dangers that threaten me
and warn me of those to come;
you withdraw me from sin and inspire me to good;
you exhort me to penance when I fall
and reconcile me to God.

I beg you not to leave me.
Comfort me in adversity,
restrain me in prosperity,
defend me in danger,
and assist me in temptations,
lest at any time I fall beneath them.
Offer up in the sight of the Divine Majesty
my prayers and petitions,
and all my works of piety,
and help me to persevere in grace
until I come to everlasting life.

## –11–

# Devotions to Saints

## Litany of the Saints

LORD, have mercy.
*Christ, have mercy.*
Lord, have mercy.
Christ, hear us.
*Christ, graciously hear us.*
God the Father of Heaven, *have mercy on us.*
God the Son, Redeemer of the world, *have mercy on us.*

God the Holy Spirit,
*have mercy on us.*
Holy Trinity, one God,
*have mercy on us.*
Holy Mary, *pray for us.**
Holy Mother of God,
Holy Virgin of virgins,
Saint Michael,
Saint Gabriel,
Saint Raphael,
All you holy Angels and Archangels,
All you holy orders of blessed spirits,
Saint John the Baptist,
Saint Joseph,
All you holy Patriarchs and Prophets,
Saint Peter,
Saint Paul,
Saint Andrew,
Saint James,
Saint John,
Saint Thomas,
Saint James,
Saint Philip,
Saint Bartholomew,
Saint Matthew,
Saint Simon,
Saint Thaddeus,
Saint Matthias,
Saint Barnabas,
Saint Luke,
Saint Mark,
All you holy Apostles and Evangelists,
All you holy Disciples of the Lord,

* *Pray for us* is repeated after each invocation down to *All you holy Virgins and Widows.*

All you holy Innocents,
Saint Stephen,
Saint Lawrence,
Saint Vincent,
Saints Fabian and Sebastian,
Saints John and Paul,
Saints Cosmas and Damian,
Saints Gervase and Protase,
All you holy Martyrs,
Saint Sylvester,
Saint Gregory,
Saint Ambrose,
Saint Augustine,
Saint Jerome,
Saint Martin,
Saint Nicholas,
All you holy Bishops and Confessors,
All you holy Doctors,
Saint Anthony,
Saint Benedict,
Saint Bernard,
Saint Dominic,
Saint Francis,
All you holy Priests and Levites,
All you holy Monks and Hermits,
Saint Mary Magdalene,
Saint Agatha,
Saint Lucy,
Saint Agnes,
Saint Cecilia,
Saint Catherine,
Saint Anastasia,
All you holy Virgins and Widows,
All you holy Men and Women, Saints of God,
*make intercession for us.*

## Prayer to Saint Patrick

Patron of Ireland

APOSTLE sent by God to Ireland,
in your humility you called yourself a sinner,
but you became a most successful missionary
and prompted countless pagans
to follow the Savior.
Many of their descendants in turn
spread the Good News in numerous foreign lands.
Through your powerful intercession with God,
obtain the missionaries we need
to continue the work you began.

## Prayer for God's Protection and Christ's Presence

AS I arise today,
may the strength of God pilot me,
the power of God uphold me,
the wisdom of God guide me.
May the eye of God look before me,
the ear of God hear me,
the word of God speak for me.
May the hand of God protect me,
the way of God lie before me,
the shield of God defend me,
the host of God save me.

May Christ shield me today . . .
Christ with me, Christ before me,
Christ behind me,
Christ in me,
Christ beneath me,
Christ above me,

Christ on my right, Christ on my left,
Christ when I lie down, Christ when I sit,
Christ when I stand,
Christ in the heart of everyone
who thinks of me,
Christ in the mouth of everyone
who speaks of me,
Christ in every eye that sees me,
Christ in every ear that hears me.

*St. Patrick of Ireland (385-461)*
Bishop and Missionary

## Prayer to Saint Francis of Assisi

Patron of Italy

DEAR Saint Francis, once worldly and vain,
you became humble and poor
for the sake of Jesus
and had an extraordinary love for the Crucified,
which showed itself in your body
by the imprints of Christ's Sacred Wounds.

In our selfish and sensual age,
how greatly we need your secret
that draws countless men and women to imitate you.
Teach us also great love for the poor
and unswerving loyalty to the Vicar of Christ.

## Prayer for the Grace to Help Others

LORD, make me an instrument of Your peace.
Where there is hatred, let me sow love.
Where there is injury, let me sow pardon.
Where there is friction, let me sow union.
Where there is error, let me sow truth.
Where there is doubt, let me sow faith.

Where there is despair, let me sow hope.
Where there is darkness, let me sow light.
Where there is sadness, let me sow joy.

O Divine Master,
grant that I may not so much seek
to be consoled as to console,
to be understood as to understand,
to be loved as to love.
For it is in giving that we receive.
It is in pardoning that we are pardoned.
It is in dying that we are born to eternal life.

*St. Francis of Assisi (1182-1226)*
Religious and Mystic

## Prayer in Praise of God for All His Creatures

MOST high, most powerful and good Lord,
to You be given praise, glory, honor,
and every blessing;
to You alone they are due, Most High,
and no one is worthy to call Your Name.

Blest be You, my Lord, with all Your creatures,
especially my lord and brother Sun,
who makes the day and by whom You give us light;
he is beautiful, radiant with great splendor:
of You, Most High, he is the symbol.

Blest be You, my Lord, for sister Moon and the Stars;
in heaven You formed them,
clear, precious, and beautiful.

Blest be You, my Lord, for brother Wind,
and for the air and the clouds,

for the calm azure and all times
by which You give sustenance to Your creatures.

Blest be You, our Lord, for sister Water,
which is very useful and humble
and precious and chaste.

Blest be You, my Lord, for brother Fire
by which You give light to the night:
it is beautiful and joyful,
unconquerable and strong.
Blest be You, my Lord, for our sister and mother Earth,
which carries and feeds us,
which produces a variety of fruits,
and variegated flowers and herbs.

Blest be You, my Lord, for those
who give pardon for love of You;
who bear trials and illnesses;
blest are they when they preserve peace
for by You, Most High, they will be crowned.

Blest be You, my Lord, for our sister bodily Death,
from whom no living person can escape;
but woe to those who die in mortal sin.
Blest those whom she will find in Your most holy Will,
for the second death will not be able to harm them.

Praise and bless my Lord,
render thanks to Him and serve Him
with great humility!

*St. Francis of Assisi (1182-1226)*
Religious and Mystic

## Prayer in Praise of God's Ineffable Greatness

YOU are holy,
O Lord and only God.
You Who work wonders.

You are strong, great, and sovereign,
You are almighty,
O Father most holy,
King of heaven and earth.
You are Triune and One at the same time,
Lord God,
and all good.
You are good, all good, and the supreme good,
O Lord God,
living and true.

You are charity and wisdom,
humility and patience,
security and tranquility,
gaiety and joy.

You are justice and temperance,
riches that surpass all sufficiency,
beauty and goodness.

You are a protector, a guardian, and a defender.
You are strength.
You are our refreshment and our courage.

You are our faith, hope, and charity.
You are our great tenderness.
You are our eternal life,

O great and wonderful Lord,
God almighty,
and dear Savior,
full of mercy.

*St. Francis of Assisi (1182-1226)*
Religious and Mystic

## Saint Peregrine
## Patron of Cancer Patients

SAINT Peregrine, whom Holy Mother Church has declared patron of those suffering from running sores and cancer, I confidently turn to you for aid in my present need. *(Here mention your request.)*

Lest I lose confidence, I beg your kind intercession. Plead with Mary, the Mother of Sorrows, whom you loved so tenderly and in union with whom you have suffered the pains of cancer, that she may help me with her all-powerful prayers and consolation.

Obtain for me the strength to accept my trials from the loving hand of God with patience and resignation. May suffering lead me to a better life and enable me to atone for my own sins and the sins of the world.

Saint Peregrine, help me to imitate you in bearing whatever cross God may permit to come to me, uniting myself with Jesus Crucified and the Mother of Sorrows. I offer my sufferings to God with all the love of my heart, for His glory and the salvation of souls, especially my own. Amen.

## Prayer

GOD, graciously hear the prayers which I present to You in honor of Saint Peregrine, Your beloved servant and devoted friend of Jesus Crucified and Our Mother of Sorrows, so that I may receive help in my needs through the intercession of him whose life had been so pleasing to You.

You filled Saint Peregrine with the spirit of compassion. Grant that by practicing works of charity I may deserve to be numbered among the elect in Your Kingdom. I ask this through Christ our Lord. Amen.

## Saint Dymphna
## Patron of the Emotionally Ill

SAINT Dymphna, a great wonderworker in every affliction of mind and body, I humbly implore your powerful intercession with Jesus through Mary, the Health of the Sick.

You are filled with love and compassion for the thousands of patients brought to your shrine for centuries, and for those who cannot come to your shrine but invoke you in their own homes or in hospitals. Show the same love and compassion toward me, your faithful client. The many miracles and cures which have been wrought through your intercession give me great confidence that you will help me in my present need. *(Here mention your request.)*

I am confident of obtaining my request, if it is for the greater glory of God and the good of my soul. For the sake of Jesus and Mary, whom you loved so earnestly, and for whom you offered your life in martyrdom, grant my prayer.

Saint Dymphna, young and beautiful, innocent and pure, help me to imitate your love of purity. You chose to be martyred by your own father's sword rather than consent to sin. Give me strength and courage in fighting off the temptations of the world and evil desires.

As you have given all the love of your heart to Jesus, help me to love God with my whole heart and serve Him faithfully. As you bore the persecution of your father and the sufferings of an exile so patiently, obtain for me the patience I need to accept the trials of my life with loving resignation to the will of God.

Saint Dymphna, through your glorious martyrdom for the love of Christ, help me to be loyal to my faith and my God as long as I live. And when the hour of my own death comes, stand at my side and pray for me that I may at last merit the eternal crown of glory in God's Kingdom.

Good Saint Dymphna, I beg you to recommend my request to Mary, the Health of the Sick and Comforter of the Afflicted, that both Mary and you may present it to Jesus, the Divine Physician.

## Prayer

O GOD, You gave Saint Dymphna to Your Church as a model of all virtues, especially holy purity, and willed that she should seal her faith with her innocent blood and perform numerous miracles. Grant that we who honor her as patroness of those afflicted with nervous and mental illness may continue to enjoy her powerful intercession and protection and attain eternal life. We ask this through Christ our Lord. Amen.

## Saint Anthony of Padua the Wonderworker

SAINT Anthony, glorious for the fame of your miracles, obtain for me from God's mercy this favor that I desire. *(Here mention your request.)*

Since you were so gracious to poor sinners, do not regard my lack of virtue but consider the glory of God which will be exalted once more through you by the granting of the petition that I now earnestly present to you.

Glorious Wonderworker, Saint Anthony, father of the poor and comforter of the afflicted, I ask for your help. You have come to my aid with such loving care and have comforted me so generously. I offer you my heartfelt thanks.

Accept this offering of my devotion and love and with it my earnest promise which I now renew, to live always in the love of God and my neighbor. Continue to shield me graciously with your protection, and obtain for me the grace of being able one day to enter the Kingdom of heaven, there to praise with you the everlasting mercies of God. Amen.

## Litany of Saint Anthony

(For Private Devotion)

LORD, have mercy.
*Christ, have mercy.*
Lord, have mercy.
Christ, hear us.
*Christ, graciously hear us.*
Holy Mary, pray for us.

Saint Francis,*
Saint Anthony of Padua,
Glory of the Order of Friars Minor,
Martyr in desiring to die for Christ,
Pillar of the Church,
Worthy priest of God,
Apostolic preacher,
Teacher of truth,
Conqueror of heretics,
Terror of evil spirits,
Comforter of the afflicted,
Helper in necessities,
Guide of the erring,
Restorer of lost things,
Chosen intercessor,
Continuous worker of miracles,
Be merciful to us, *spare us, O Lord.*
Be merciful to us, *hear us, O Lord.*
From all evil, *deliver us, O Lord.*
From all sin,**
From all dangers of body and soul,
From the snares of the devil,
From pestilence, famine, and war,
From eternal death,
Through the merits of Saint Anthony,
Through his zeal for the conversion of sinners,
Through his desire for the crown of martyrdom,
Through his fatigues and labors,
Through his preaching and teaching,
Through his penitential tears,
Through his patience and humility,

* *Pray for us* is repeated after each invocation down to *Be merciful to us.*

** *Deliver us, O Lord* is repeated after each invocation down to *In the day of judgment.*

Through his glorious death,
Through the number of his prodigies,
In the day of judgment,
We sinners, *we beseech You, hear us,*
That You would bring us to true penance,***
That You would grant us patience in our trials,
That You would assist us in our necessities,
That You would hear our prayers and petitions,
That You would kindle the fires of Divine love within us,
That You would grant us the protection and intercession of Saint Anthony,
Son of God,
Lamb of God, You take away the sins of the world; *spare us, O Lord.*
Lamb of God, You take away the sins of the world; *graciously hear us, O Lord.*
Lamb of God, You take away the sins of the world; *have mercy on us.*
Christ, hear us.
*Christ, graciously hear us.*
℣. Pray for us, O blessed Saint Anthony.
℟. *That we may be made worthy of the promises of Christ.*

## Prayer

ALMIGHTY and eternal God, You glorified Your faithful confessor Anthony with the perpetual gift of working miracles. Grant that what we confidently seek through his merits we may surely receive by his intercession. We ask this in the Name of Jesus the Lord.

℟. *Amen.*

*** *We beseech You, hear us,* is repeated after each invocation down to *Son of God.*

## Saint Thérèse of the Child Jesus Patroness of Missionaries

SAINT Thérèse of the Child Jesus, during your short life on earth you became a mirror of angelic purity, of love strong as death, and of wholehearted abandonment to God. Now that you rejoice in the reward of your virtue, turn your eyes of mercy upon me, for I put all my confidence in you.

Obtain for me the grace to keep my heart and mind pure and clean like your own, and to abhor sincerely whatever may in any way tarnish the glorious virtue of purity, so dear to our Lord.

Most gracious Little Rose Queen, remember your promises of never letting any request made to you go unanswered, of sending down a shower of roses, and of coming down to earth to do good. Full of confidence in your power with the Sacred Heart, I implore your intercession in my behalf and beg of you to obtain the request I so ardently desire. *(Here mention your request.)*

Holy "Little Thérèse," remember your promise "to do good upon earth" and shower down your "roses" on those who invoke you. Obtain for me from God the graces I hope for from His infinite goodness. Let me feel the power of your prayers in every need. Give me consolation in all the bitterness of this life, and especially at the hour of death, that I may be worthy to share eternal happiness with you in heaven. Amen.

## Prayer

FATHER in heaven, through Saint Thérèse of the Child Jesus, You desire to remind the world of the merciful love that fills Your Heart and the childlike trust we should have in You. Humbly we thank You for having crowned with such great glory Your ever-faithful child and for giving her wondrous power to bring to You, day by day, innumerable souls who will praise You eternally.

O Lord, You said, "Unless you . . . become like little children, you shall not enter the Kingdom of heaven" (Mt 18:3); grant us, we beg of You, to walk in the footsteps of Your virgin, Saint Theresa, with humility and purity of intention so that we may obtain eternal rewards. You live and reign forever. Amen.

## Saint Jude Thaddeus Novena Prayer

GLORIOUS Saint Jude Thaddeus, by those sublime privileges with which you were adorned in your lifetime, namely, your relationship with our Lord Jesus Christ according to the flesh, and your vocation to be an Apostle, and by that glory which now is yours in heaven as the reward of your apostolic labors and your martyrdom, obtain for me from the Giver of every good and perfect gift all the graces of which I stand in need. *(Here mention your request.)*

May I treasure up in my heart the divinely inspired doctrines that you have given us in your Epistle: to build my edifice of holiness upon our most holy faith, by praying for the grace of the Holy Spirit; to keep myself in the love of God, looking for the mercy of Jesus Christ unto eternal life; to strive by all means to help those who go astray.

May I thus praise the glory and majesty, the dominion and power of Him Who is able to keep me without sin and to present me spotless with great joy at the coming of our Divine Savior, the Lord Jesus Christ. Amen.

## Consecration to Saint Jude

SAINT Jude, Apostle of Christ and glorious martyr, I desire to honor you with a special devotion. I choose you as my patron and protector. To you I entrust my soul and my body, all my spiritual and temporal interests, as well as those of my family. To you I consecrate my mind so that in all things it may be enlightened by faith; my heart so that you may keep it pure and fill it with love for Jesus and Mary; my will so that, like yours, it may always be one with the Will of God.

I beg you to help me to master my evil inclinations and temptations and to avoid all occasions of sin. Obtain for me the grace of never offending God, of fulfilling faithfully all the duties of my state of life, and of practicing all those virtues that are needful for my salvation.

Pray for me, my holy patron and helper, so that, being inspired by your example and assisted by your prayers, I may live a holy life, die a happy death, and attain to the glory of heaven, there to love and thank God forever. Amen.

### Prayer

O GOD, You made Your Name known to us through the Apostles. By the intercession of Saint Jude, let Your Church continue to grow with an increased number of believers. Grant this through Christ our Lord. Amen.

*–12–*

## Devotions for the Faithful Departed

### Prayers for the Holy Souls

THE CHURCH encourages us to pray for the dead—either through liturgical prayers (like the Eucharist and the Liturgy of the Hours) or through private prayers (like those found in this section). She reminds us that it is a holy and wholesome thought to pray for the dead that they may be loosed from their sins.

The Second Vatican Council upheld the time-honored custom of praying for the dead: "Very much aware of the bonds linking the whole Mystical Body of Jesus Christ, the pilgrim Church from the very first ages of the Christian religion has cultivated with great piety the memory of the dead. Because it is 'a holy and wholesome thought to pray for the dead that they may be loosed from sins' (2 Mac 12:46), she has also offered prayers for them. . . .

Hence, we who are still able to increase the Divine life in us, still able to win God's favor by our cooperation with the grace of Christ, can help the suffering members of God's family, who are in purgatory. They in turn can and do pray for us—although they cannot help themselves.

The prayers in this section are intended to foster this laudable devotion to the holy souls in purgatory and to provide models for other prayers to be drawn up. At the same time, such devotion is an apt reminder of our own death and the need to be ready for it by living in a truly Christian fashion.

## Prayer to the Father for All the Faithful Departed

HEAVENLY Father
I believe that in Your wisdom and justice
You willed to purify all persons who die
without having attained the state that they need
for all eternity,
all who have still to expiate completely
the sins committed on earth.
I also believe that You have mercifully arranged
that this process of purification can be aided
by the prayers of the living,
and especially by the Eucharist.

Help me to pray for my brothers and sisters
who have departed from this world.
May their time of purification be short
and they be quickly guided into that holy light
promised by our Lord to Abraham and his descendants.
I offer You sacrifices and prayers of praise.
Accept them for all the souls of the faithful departed
and admit them all to the eternal joy of heaven.

## Prayer to Jesus and Mary for All the Faithful Departed

MOST loving Jesus,
I humbly beg You to offer to Your eternal Father
in behalf of the holy souls in purgatory,
the most Precious Blood that poured forth
from the sacred wounds of Your adorable Body,
together with Your Agony and Death.
O sorrowful Virgin Mary,
do you also present to the Father,
together with the dolorous Passion of your Son,
your own sighs and tears
and all the sorrows you suffered in His suffering,
in order that through the merits of the same,
the souls now suffering in purgatory
may receive refreshment and peace.
Delivered from that painful state,
may they be clothed with glory in heaven,
there to sing the glories of God for ever and ever.

## Prayer to Jesus for the Suffering Souls

MY JESUS,
by the sorrows You suffered
in Your Agony in the Garden,
in the Scourging and Crowning with Thorns,
in the Way to Calvary,
in Your Crucifixion and Death,
have mercy on the souls in purgatory,
especially those who are most forsaken.
Deliver them from the dire torments they endure,
and admit them to Your most sweet embrace in paradise.

*Our Father. Hail Mary. Eternal rest, etc.*

## Prayer for a Departed Father and Mother

GOD,
You commanded us to honor father and mother.
In Your goodness,
have mercy on the souls of my father and mother
(*or* the soul of my father, *or* the soul of my mother),
and forgive them their sins
(*or* forgive him his sins, *or* forgive her her sins),
and bring me to see them (*or* him, *or* her)
in the joy of eternal happiness.
We ask this through Christ our Lord.

## Prayer for Departed Relatives, Friends and Benefactors

HEAVENLY Father
accept my prayer for all those in purgatory
for whom I should pray because of ties
of family, gratitude, justice, or charity.
Have mercy on my relatives, friends, and benefactors
as well as those who held positions of authority,
both civil and religious.
Admit them all to Your eternal happiness in heaven.
Eternal rest grant to them, O Lord.
And let perpetual light shine upon them.
May they rest in peace.

## Prayers of Saint Gertrude for the Faithful Departed

### Introductory Prayer

HAIL, Jesus Christ, Splendor of the Father;
hail, Prince of peace, Gate of heaven,
Living Bread, Offspring of the Virgin,
and Vessel of the Godhead.
Eternal rest grant to them, O Lord.
And let perpetual light shine upon them.

### First Prayer

I ADORE, greet, and bless You,
O Lord Jesus Christ.
I praise You and give You thanks
with the love of all Your creatures
for the infinite love that led You
to become Man for us,
to be born and endure hunger and thirst,
toils and sorrows for thirty-three years,
and to bestow Yourself upon us
in the Most Holy Sacrament.

I beg You to unite my prayer
with Your most holy conversation and life
on behalf of *N.* departed
(*or* all the faithful departed).
Supply from the great abundance of Your merits
for the things in which he/she is lacking.
Perfectly complete whatever he/she neglected
in Your worship and love,
in thanksgiving and prayer,
in virtue and good works,
and all the service due to You,

in all that by Your grace he/she might have done
and has not done,
or did from impure motives or carelessly and imperfectly.

## Second Prayer

I ADORE, greet, and bless You,
O Lord Jesus Christ.
I give You thanks for that love by which You,
the Creator of all things,
willed for our redemption to be
seized and bound and dragged away to judgment,
trampled upon, buffeted, and spit upon,
scourged and crowned with thorns,
condemned to bear Your own Cross,
stripped and nailed to the Cross,
die a most bitter death,
and be pierced through with a lance.

In union with that love,
I offer You my unworthy prayers,
begging You to blot out and utterly efface
through the merits of Your Passion and Death
whatever this departed person for whom I pray
has ever done against Your Will
by evil thoughts, or words, or deeds.
I ask that You offer to the Father
all the sorrow and anguish of Your torn Body
and of Your desolated Soul,
all Your merits and all Your actions,
for all the chastisement that he/she has incurred
at the hands of Your justice.

## Third Prayer

I ADORE, greet, and bless You,
O Lord Jesus Christ.
I give You thanks for all the love and faithfulness
with which You overcame death and rose from the dead,
and glorified our flesh by ascending in it
to the right hand of the Father.
I beg You to enable the soul for whom I pray
to be a partaker of Your triumph and glory.

## Fourth Prayer

I ADORE, greet, and bless You,
O Lord Jesus Christ.
I render You thanks for all the graces
that You have ever bestowed on Your glorious Mother
and on all the Elect,
in union with the gratitude
with which all Your Saints exult in the bliss
that You have obtained for them
through Your holy Incarnation, Passion, and Resurrection.
I beg You to supply to this departed person,
from the merits and prayers of the same glorious Virgin
and all Your Saints,
whatever is lacking to his/her own.

## Litany for the Souls in Purgatory

(For Private Devotion)

LORD, have mercy.
*Christ, have mercy.*

Lord, have mercy.
Christ, hear us.
*Christ, graciously hear us.*
God the Father of heaven, *have mercy on the suffering souls.*
God the Son, Redeemer of the world, *have mercy on the suffering souls.*
God the Holy Spirit, *have mercy on the suffering souls.*
Holy Trinity, one God, *have mercy on the suffering souls.*
Holy Mary, *pray for the suffering souls.**
Holy Mother of God,
Holy Virgin of virgins,
Saint Michael,
All you holy Angels and Archangels,
All you holy orders of blessed spirits,
Saint John the Baptist,
Saint Joseph,
All you holy Patriarchs and Prophets,
Saint Peter,
Saint Paul,
Saint John,
All you holy Apostles and Evangelists,
Saint Stephen,
Saint Lawrence,
All you holy Martyrs,
Saint Gregory,
Saint Ambrose,
Saint Augustine,
Saint Jerome,
All you holy Bishops and Confessors,
All you holy Doctors,

* *Pray for the suffering souls* is repeated after each invocation.

All you holy Priests and Levites,
All you holy Monks and Hermits,
Saint Mary Magdalene,
Saint Catherine,
Saint Barbara,
All you holy Virgins and Widows,
All you holy men and women, Saints of God.
Be merciful to them, *spare them, O Lord.*
Be merciful to them, *graciously hear us, O Lord.*
From all suffering, *deliver them, O Lord.***
From all delay,
From the rigor of Your justice,
From the gnawing pain of conscience,
From fearful darkness,
From their mourning and tears,
Through the mystery of Your Incarnation,
Through Your Coming,
Through Your Nativity,
Through Your own sweet Name,
Through Your Baptism and holy Fasting,
Through Your most profound humility,
Through Your perfect submission,
Through Your infinite love,
Through Your anguish and torment,
Through Your bloody sweat,
Through Your bonds and chains,
Through Your Crown of Thorns,
Through Your ignominious Death,
Through Your sacred Wounds,
Through Your Cross and bitter Passion,
Through Your glorious Resurrection,
Through Your admirable Ascension,
Through Your coming of the Holy Spirit, the Paraclete,

** *Deliver them, O Lord* is repeated after each invocation.

In the day of judgment, *we beseech You, hear us.****

We sinners,

You Who absolved the adulteress and pardoned the good thief,

You Who save by Your grace,

You Who have the keys of death and of hell,

That You would deign to deliver our parents, friends, and benefactors from torments,

That You would deign to deliver all the faithful departed,

That You would deign to have mercy on all those who have none in this world to remember or pray for them,

That You would deign to have mercy on all and to deliver them from their pains,

That You would deign to fulfill their desires,

That You would deign to admit them among Your Elect,

King of dreadful majesty,

Son of God,

Lamb of God, You take away the sins of the world; *give them rest.*

Lamb of God, You take away the sins of the world; *give them rest.*

Lamb of God, You take away the sins of the world; *give them eternal rest.*

Jesus Christ, hear us.

Jesus Christ, *graciously hear us.*

From the fate of hell,

*O Lord, You have delivered them.*

*** *We beseech You, hear us* is repeated after each invocation.

Let us pray.
O Lord,
the Creator and Redeemer of all the faithful,
grant to the souls of Your faithful departed
the remission of all their sins.
By the supplications of Your Church
may they obtain the pardon
that they have always desired from Your mercy,
Who live forever and ever.

## Invocations

MY GOD,
pour forth Your blessings and Your mercies upon all persons
and upon all souls in purgatory for whom,
by reason of charity, gratitude, and friendship,
I am bound or desire to pray.

JESUS, our Savior,
give us Your blessing,
deliver us from everlasting death,
assist Your holy Church,
give peace to all nations,
and deliver the holy souls suffering in purgatory.

ETERNAL rest grant to them,
O Lord,
and let perpetual light shine upon them.
May they rest in peace.

MARY, Mother of God and Mother of mercy,
pray for us and for all who have died
in the embrace of the Lord.

HOLY Mary,
our Lady of Deliverance,
pray for us
and for the holy souls in purgatory.

## Prayers for the Faithful Departed for Every Day of the Week

### Sunday

O LORD God almighty,
I beg You,
by the Precious Blood that Your Divine Son shed in the Garden:
deliver the souls in purgatory,
and especially the soul among them
that is most destitute of spiritual aid.

Be pleased to bring that soul into Your glory,
there to praise and bless You forever.

*Our Father. Hail Mary. Eternal rest, etc.*

### Monday

O LORD God almighty,
I beg You,
by the Precious Blood that Your Divine Son
shed in His cruel Scourging:
deliver the souls in purgatory,
and the soul especially among them
that is nearest to its entrance into Your glory—
so that it may immediately begin to praise and bless You
and continue to do so forever.

*Our Father. Hail Mary. Eternal rest, etc.*

## Tuesday

O LORD God almighty Father,
I beg You,
by the Precious Blood that Your Divine Son shed
in His bitter Crowning with Thorns:
deliver the souls in purgatory,
and in particular the one among them
that would be the last to depart from it—
so that this soul may not tarry so long a time
before coming to praise You in Your glory
and bless You forever.

*Our Father. Hail Mary. Eternal rest, etc.*

## Wednesday

O LORD God almighty,
I beg You,
by the Precious Blood that Your Divine Son shed
in the streets of Jerusalem
when He carried the Cross upon His sacred shoulders:
deliver the souls in purgatory,
and especially the soul that is richest in merits
in Your sight.
May that soul attain the awaiting throne of glory
and magnify and bless You forever.

*Our Father. Hail Mary. Eternal rest, etc.*

## Thursday

O LORD God almighty,
I beg You,
by the Precious Blood of Your Divine Son,

that He gave with His own hands
upon the eve of His Passion to His beloved Apostles
to be their meat and drink,
and that He left to the whole Church
to be a perpetual sacrifice
and the life-giving Food of His own faithful people:
deliver the souls in purgatory,
and especially the one that was most devoted
to this Mystery of infinite love.

May that soul in union with Your Divine Son
and Your Holy Spirit
ever praise You for Your love therein
in eternal glory.

*Our Father. Hail Mary. Eternal rest, etc.*

## Friday

O LORD God almighty,
I beg You,
by the Precious Blood, that Your Divine Son shed
on the wood of the Cross on this day,
especially from His sacred hands and feet:
deliver the souls in purgatory,
and in particular that soul
for which I am most bound to pray.
May no neglect of mine ever hinder that soul
from praising You in Your glory
and blessing You forever.

*Our Father. Hail Mary. Eternal rest, etc.*

### Saturday

O LORD God almighty,
I beg You,
by the Precious Blood that gushed from the side
of Your Divine Son
in the sight of and to the extreme pain of
His most holy Mother:
deliver the souls in purgatory,
and especially the one among them
that was most devoted to her.
May that soul soon attain Your glory,
there to praise You—and her in You—forever.

*Our Father. Hail Mary. Eternal rest, etc.*

## –13–

# Devotions for Personal Needs

### Healing Meditation

NOTHING in nature happens by chance. All creatures have a reason for their existence. There is also a reason for the existence of pain in the world, otherwise God would never permit it.

It is not for us to question God's Divine plan. Our duty is to accept life with its sorrows and joys willingly. As creatures we are bound to God, our Creator. He did not abandon us after bringing us into this life, and He does not intend to do so. We must pray for faith that we may be able to fit the stark realities of life into His Divine plan. Our daily trials cannot harm us unless we rebel against them and God's plan.

Suffering, sadness, and cares come to us to remind us that earth is not a paradise and that the life, truth, and love we crave are not to be found here below. The possession of God is our end in life, as Saint Augustine wrote: "You have made us for Yourself, Lord, and our hearts are restless until they rest in You."

Jesus is our model of suffering willingly. Bodily suffering, mental anguish, bitter disappointment, the false judgment of justice, the betrayal of true friendship, the court's perversion of honesty, and the violent separation from a mother's love—all these Jesus took upon Himself knowingly, freely, and willingly. Then after the Crucifixion, He uttered a word of triumph, "It is finished" (Jn 19:30).

It was all according to His Father's plan. On the Cross the plan was finished. Its full meaning was not revealed until three days later, when the Seed that fell to the ground arose into the newness of Life. It was this plan Jesus gave to the disciples on the way to Emmaus, "Was it not necessary that the Messiah should suffer these things and enter into His glory?" (Lk 24:26).

Suffering, then, has a part in our Father's plan. Sickness can be the cause of much suffering, but Jesus said, "Come to Me, all you who are weary and overburdened, and I will give you rest. Take My yoke upon you and learn from Me, for I am meek and humble of heart, and you will find rest for your souls. For My yoke is easy and My burden light" (Mt 11:28-30). "Amen, amen, I say to you, if you ask the Father anything in My Name, He will give it to you" (Jn 16:23).

It is God's Will that you pray and in this way His promise will be fulfilled, "Ask, and it will be given you; seek, and you will find; knock, and the door will be opened to you" (Lk 11:9). Therefore, it is right to pray for good health.

## THE WORD OF GOD

"You will weep and mourn while the world rejoices. You will be sorrowful, but your grief will turn into joy … and no one shall deprive you of your joy." *John 16:20-22*

"But rejoice insofar as you are sharing in the sufferings of Christ, so that your joy will be without limit when his glory is revealed." *1 Peter 4:13*

"God is faithful, and he will not allow you to be tried beyond your strength. But together with the trial he will also provide a way out and the strength to bear it." *1 Corinthians 10:13*

"Ask, and it will be given you; seek, and you will find; knock, and the door will be opened to you." *Luke 11:9*

## Novena Prayer

JESUS, Divine Physician, You have created nature and all the wondrous functions of the human body. You are the Master of Your creation. You can and do suspend the laws of nature for those who have faith in Your goodness and entreat You in fervent prayer. You said, "Ask, and it will be given you; seek, and you will find; knock, and the door will be opened to you"

(Lk 11:9). Full of confidence in this promise, I beg You to help me in my present need. (*Here mention your request.*)

Jesus, during Your lifetime You cured sickness and disease and even raised the dead to life, because people asked You to do so in prayer. I firmly believe that You will hear my prayer also, if this should be the Will of God.

I ask for the grace to understand more and more the infinite love of Your Sacred Heart for me. I firmly believe that You love me with a love that ordains all things for my own good even though this may be difficult for my nature to bear. It is a love that turns to good all that I may at the moment consider evil. I love Your Heart that loves me so much.

Jesus, my Savior, I thank You for being my best Friend in any illness of my life and my Companion in suffering: I thank You for loving me with a Heart human like my own—a Heart that can understand my sorrows and problems since It has experienced all that I must bear; a Heart that can sympathize with me and befriend me in my hour of need; a Heart that can love me with the love of the best of friends. Your Heart burns for me with a love that knows no end because It has its source in the depths of the Godhead. Not all the affection You pour out upon countless other souls lessens Your love for me.

Jesus, I unite myself with You as You offer yourself during the Holy Sacrifice of the Mass and renew Your Sacrifice of Calvary. Give my heart sentiments like Your own, so that through frequent Holy Communion and prayer I may become holy and pleasing to God, a worthy sacrifice with You. May all the actions, sufferings, tears, and disappointments of my life be thus consecrated to You as a sacrifice for the glory of God.

Give me the grace to bear cheerfully and willingly everything that You send me, or permit in my life, whether favorable or unfavorable, for I am resolved to conform myself to the Divine Will in all things. May God's Will always be my will! Amen.

## Prayer to Our Lady, Health of the Sick

MY DEAREST Mother Mary, I confidently invoke you as the Health of the Sick. You are the loving Mother especially of those who are blessed with a cross, particularly illness. I humbly plead for this favor. (*Here mention your request.*)

Mother of Perpetual Help, I beg you to present my petition to your Divine Son. If you will pray for me, I cannot be refused, for your prayers before God are powerful. With childlike trust I abandon myself to God's holy Will concerning my request.

Mother of Mercy, I love you; I put all my confidence in you. I offer to God through your hands every suffering that I must bear, with all the love of my heart. Make every pain an act of love for God, an act of atonement for my sins, and meritorious for the salvation of souls, especially for my own soul. Teach me patience and resignation to the holy Will of God, in imitation of you, dear Mother of Sorrows.

℣. Pray for us, Our Lady, Health of the Sick.
℟. *That we may be made worthy of the promises of Christ.*

Let us pray. Grant us, Your servants, we beg You, Lord God, that we may be blessed with health of soul and body, and by the glorious intercession of the Blessed Virgin Mary, Health of the Sick, be freed from the sorrows of this present life and enjoy everlasting bliss. We ask this through Christ our Lord. Amen.

## Prayer for Patience in Sickness

HEAVENLY Father, Your Son accepted our sufferings to teach us the virtue of patience in human illness. Hear my prayer and help me in my sufferings. May I realize that You have chosen me to be a Saint through my sufferings and that I am joined to Christ in His suffering for the salvation of the world.

Show me the power of Your loving care and restore my health, if it be Your Will, that I may offer joyful thanks in Your Church.

Direct my heart and body in the love of You and the patience of Christ. Help me, defend me from all evil and bring me safely to life everlasting.

Heavenly Father, Your Will be done!

# Novena for Our Family

## Meditation

THE calling of every family is to share life together with a deep, personal love according to God's Will. It is the family's calling to become a community, sharing life together in deep love and respect for each other. The family is the most sacred of all societies. Our character, beliefs, thoughts, and virtues come from good loving parents.

Family life has this aim: that the spouses be ready with generous hearts to work together with the love of the Creator Who through them will enlarge and enrich His own family day by day.

Marriage is a lifelong partnership of love. The giving of self in marriage brings children who make the love of husbands and wives richer and fulfills one of the purposes of marriage. If husbands and wives are generous to God in working with Him according to His Will, enlarging His own family on earth, He will bless them in this life and especially in heaven.

This blessing of God can be expressed in the form of the Eight Beatitudes, given to us by Jesus in His Sermon on the Mount. There are Eight Beatitudes for the Home.

1. Blessed is the home where the father, mother, and children love God sincerely and keep His commandments faithfully, go to Confession regularly, receive Holy Communion frequently, and pray much; for the Lord lives in such a home.

2. Blessed is the home in which the Sundays and holy days are properly observed, for the members will one day meet again at the festival of heaven.

3. Blessed is the home which no one leaves to go to sinful amusements, for in it the joy of Christ shall reign.

4. Blessed is the home where unkind speech does not enter, nor cursing, nor bad literature, nor intemperance, for on that home will be heaped the blessings of peace.

5. Blessed is the home where father and mother are conscious of the sacred dignity of bringing children into the world and educating them in the service of God, where they faithfully fulfill the obligations they have toward each other and their children, and detest the sins sometimes committed in the married state, for they will merit the favor and abundant blessings of God.

6. Blessed is the home to which a priest is called in time and often to attend the sick, for their illness will have its consolation and death will be happy.

7. Blessed is the home where Christian doctrine is properly appreciated and learned from the catechism and good books, for in that home the faith will be kept firm and active.

8. Blessed is the home where the parents find their joy in children who are dutiful and obedient, and where the children find in their parents the example of the fear and love of God, for that home will be the home of just people, the haven of virtues, and the ark of salvation.

We must pray earnestly and often that these blessings of God come upon our family. We can do so by making an occasional novena for our family. No one deserves this more than the persons we love so dearly in our family.

## THE WORD OF GOD

"Honor your father and your mother so that your days may be lengthened in the land that the Lord your God, will give you." *Exodus 20:12*

"Blessed, are all those who fear the Lord and walk in his ways. ... Within your house; your sons will be like shoots of an olive tree around your table." *Psalms 128:1-3*

## Novena Prayer

GOD of goodness and mercy, to Your fatherly protection we commend our family, our household and all that belongs to us. We entrust all to Your love and keeping. Fill our home with Your blessings as You filled the holy House of Nazareth with Your presence.

Above all things else, keep far from us the stain of sin. We want You alone to reign over us. Help each one of us to obey Your holy laws, love You sincerely, and imitate Your example, the example of Mary, Jesus' Mother and ours, and the example of the holy guardian Saint Joseph.

Lord, preserve us and our home from all evils and misfortunes, but grant that we may be ever resigned to Your Divine Will even in the sorrows which it may please You to send, or in any cross you may permit to come to us.

Give all of us the grace to live in perfect harmony and charity toward our neighbor. Grant that every one of us may deserve by a holy life the comfort of Your holy Sacraments at the hour of death.

We also ask You to grant us this special request. *(Here mention your request.)*

Bless our home, God the Father, Who created us, God the Son, Who suffered for us upon the Cross, and God the Holy Spirit, Who sanctified us in Baptism. One God in Three Divine Persons, preserve our bodies, purify our minds, direct our hearts, and bring us all to everlasting life!

## Consecration to the Sacred Heart of Jesus

MOST Sacred Heart of Jesus, You revealed to Saint Margaret Mary Your desire to rule over Christian families. Behold, in order to please You, we consecrate our family to Your Sacred Heart and proclaim Your Reign over us.

We want to live Your life. May the Virtues to which You have promised peace on earth flower in our family. Keep far from us the spirit of the world which You have condemned.

Jesus, be the King of our minds by the simplicity of our faith. Be the King of our hearts by our love of You alone; help us to keep alive this flame of love in our hearts by receiving Holy Communion frequently and by prayer.

Sacred Heart of Jesus, be pleased to preside over us when we assemble. Bless our spiritual and temporal affairs, ward off all trouble, sanctify our joys, and give us consolation in sorrows.

If any of us should have the misfortune of offending You, Heart of Jesus, give that person the grace to remember that You are kind and merciful to the repentant sinner.

When the hour of separation strikes and death enters our family circle, whether we go or whether we stay, help us all to submit humbly to Your eternal decrees. Let it be our consolation to remember that the day will come when our entire family, once more united in heaven, will praise Your glory and goodness forever.

May the Immaculate Heart of Mary and the glorious Patriarch Saint Joseph be pleased to offer You this our act of consecration.

## Consecration to the Holy Family

JESUS, our most loving Redeemer, You came to enlighten the world with Your teaching and example. You willed to spend the greater part of Your life in humble obedience to Mary and Joseph in the poor home of Nazareth. In this way You sanctified that Family which was to be an example for all Christian families.

Graciously accept our family which we dedicate and consecrate to You. Be pleased to protect, guard, and keep it in holy fear, in peace, and in the harmony of Christian charity. By conforming ourselves to the Divine model of your Family, may we all attain to eternal happiness.

Mary, Mother of Jesus and our Mother, by your merciful intercession make this our humble offering acceptable to Jesus, and obtain for us graces and blessings.

Saint Joseph, most holy guardian of Jesus and Mary, help us by your prayers in all our spiritual and temporal needs so that we may praise Jesus our Divine Savior, together with Mary and you, for all eternity.

## Prayer

LORD, we pray that You visit our home and drive far from it all snares of the enemy. Let Your Holy Angels dwell in it to preserve us in peace; and let Your blessing be always upon us. Through the prayers of the Blessed Virgin Mary, we beg You to guard our family from all danger. And as we humbly worship You with all our hearts, in Your mercy graciously protect us from all the snares of the enemy and keep us in Your peace. We ask this through Jesus Christ our Lord. Amen.

## Petition to Jesus, Mary, and Joseph

DEAR Jesus, Mary, and Joseph, to you we consecrate our family and all that we have. We want our home to belong entirely to you. You made family life holy by your family life at Nazareth. Your home was a home of prayer, love, patient endurance, and toil.

It is our earnest wish to model our home upon yours at Nazareth. Remain with us, so that with your help the purity of our morals may be preserved, that we may obey the Commandments of God and of the Church, and receive the Sacraments frequently.

Willingly we surrender our entire freedom to you, our Queen and our Mother. We place under your care our body and its senses, our soul and its faculties, our thoughts and desires, our words and deeds, our joys and sorrows, our life and our death.

Give your aid to our family, to our relatives, and to all who do us good. Under your guidance may we always follow the Holy Spirit and never hinder His grace in us through sin.

Help us to tread our way successfully through the dangers of this life and so win passage to our home country in heaven. As Saints there with you, may we sing the praises of each Person of the Blessed Trinity for all eternity.

Keep love and peace in our midst. Console us in our troubles. Help us to preserve the innocence of our children. Enlighten and strengthen our growing sons and daughters. Assist us all at the hour of death, so that we may be united with each other and with you in heaven.

## Prayer to the Heavenly Father

FATHER, our family looks to Your loving guidance and order as the pattern of all family life. By following the example of the Holy Family of Your Son, in mutual love and respect, may we come to the joy of our home in heaven.

Father, by the power of Your Spirit You have filled the hearts of Your faithful people with gifts of love for one another. Hear the prayers I offer for our family, relatives, and benefactors. Give us health of mind and body that we may do Your Will with perfect love.

Pardon our sins. Give us Your constant encouragement and guide us throughout our lives, until the day when we, with all who have served You, will rejoice in Your presence forever in heaven. Amen.

"Let the little children come to me, and do not hinder them. For it is such as these that the kingdom of heaven belongs." *Matthew 19:14*

# PART V

# CATHOLIC BLESSINGS

## –1–

## Prayer-Blessings of People *Consecrating Them to God*

BLESSINGS have been used from time immemorial to consecrate people to God. By blessing those we love or come into contact with, we call down God's help on their mission and their needs.

*The prayers for God's blessings in this part of the book are all intended to be prayed by lay people. They aim to get people in the habit of calling upon God at every moment of their lives and to impart the conviction to them that everything has a role to play in the working out of their supernatural destiny.*

### Blessing of an Engaged Couple

HEAVENLY Father,
we praise You for Your wisdom
in arranging that man should not be alone
but should unite himself to another
to form a living cell or unit,
bringing forth new members for Your Kingdom (Mt 19:5f).

Bless this Couple who have manifested their intention
to unite in marriage in the future.
Keep them close to You and to one another,
deepen their spirit of prayer and love,
and lead them to receive the Sacrament of Marriage
with joy and happiness.
We ask this in the Name of Jesus the Lord.

## Blessing for a Wedding Anniversary

HEAVENLY Father,
Lord of the universe,
we praise You for Your goodness
in providing helpmates for human beings
that they may comfort and encourage one another
in their journey through life.
We thank You for the years together
that You have granted this Couple.

May they continue to find joy and companionship
in each other
and in union with You.
May their children revere them,
their friends esteem them,
and all human beings respect them
for their devotion to You and to one another.
We ask this through Jesus Christ our Lord.

## Blessing of a Woman before Childbirth

HEAVENLY Father and Author of life,
You are the Creator of every human soul,
but You enable a woman to conceive
and give birth to a child

that can become forever a blessed child of Yours.
We praise and thank You for this privilege.

Bless this Mother and her unborn child.
Give her courage.
Make her grateful for her privilege,
repeating with the Blessed Virgin Mary:
"God, Who is mighty, has done great things for me.
Holy is His Name!" (Lk 1:49).
Grant this through Christ our Lord.

## Blessing of a Child

DEAR Lord Jesus,
eternal Son of God,
You chose to become a little child
although You could have taken on
a fully developed nature of an adult.
You loved children for their innocence and said:
"The Kingdom of God belongs to such as these" (Lk 18:16).

Bless this Child and give it abundant grace,
that it may be true joy for the parents
and as it becomes more Christlike
it may give you ever greater glory
and serve as an example for both young and old.

## Blessing of a Sick Child

COMPASSIONATE Lord and Savior,
You know well how profound a grief is suffered
by normal mothers when their child is sick.
Good mothers are truly "compassionate,"
that is, they suffer with their children.
Please bless this Sick Child
and bring consolation to the parents.

This we ask through the intercession of Mary, our Mother,
who on Calvary became the Mother of Sorrows.

## Blessing of a Family

FATHER in heaven,
we give You thanks and praise
for instituting the human family
to multiply and fill the earth (Gen 1:28),
thus making husband and wife Your cooperators.
Bless this family
and keep them one in heart and mind (Acts 2:31).

May they take as their model
the holy Family of Nazareth in which
the Child Jesus was obedient,
Mary and Joseph were ever devoted to their tasks,
and all prayed together and stayed together.
We ask this in the Name of Jesus.

## Blessing of an Aged Person

MERCIFUL Lord,
we know that with its many good aspects,
such as wisdom and serenity,
old age also brings various ailments.
Teach this Person to meditate often
on the sufferings of Your innocent Son.

Sustain and encourage him/her to accept the crosses,
in the realization that sufferings can be offered
for the good of souls,
for conversions,
for vocations to the priesthood and the religious life.

Enable him/her to entrust himself/herself
to Your Holy Spirit, the Spirit of love,
Who is of all consolers the very best.
Grant this through our Lord Jesus Christ.

### Blessing of a Sick Person

GOD of Love,
Your Son became Man
and acted not only as a physician of souls
but also as a healer of physical and mental illnesses.
We ask You to cure this Sick Person
if it is in accord with Your plan for him/her.

Enable him/her to serve You
with a healthy body and mind.
May he/she strive for Christian perfection,
helped by Your grace,
for Your greater glory and honor
and for the advantage of his/her neighbor.

## –2–

## Prayer-Blessings of Places — *Centering the World on God*

WE BLESS places to remind ourselves of God's presence in them and of the use they can be to our salvation. Thus, our whole world can be centered on God and everything we do can redound to His greater glory.

*The subjects chosen for the blessings in this section are the most usual places in which our lives unfold in the normal course of events. The blessings can thus serve as models for blessings of other places in our experience. The most important thing to remember is that no place on earth is devoid of God's powerful presence and no place is outside the pale of the salvation wrought by Christ through the power of the Spirit.*

## Blessing of a Home

HEAVENLY Father,
Your Divine Son came to this earth
and lived for many years in a home at Nazareth (Lk 2:5)
that was sanctified by the Holy Family:
Jesus, Mary, and Joseph.
Bless this Home
and all who live or come to visit here.
May it always breathe forth the true Christian spirit,
the spirit of Your Son Who said:
"Seek first [God's] kingship over you, His way of holiness,
and everything else will be given you besides" (Mt 6:33).

At the same time, may all members of this home
also be fully human,
fully committed to their vocation
—whether secular or religious—
so that they may continue to build up
the Body of Christ here below
until He returns in glory at the end of time.

## Blessing of a School

FATHER of truth and wisdom,
we thank You for making human beings so wonderfully

and for endowing them with the limitless capacity
for intellectual, experiential, and moral learning.
We thank You for sending Your Son
as the Teacher par excellence
to teach us the way to You.
He instructed a group of unlettered disciples
and sent them out to teach all nations (Mt 28:19).
He taught them so well
that they eloquently spread His teaching
throughout the world of their day.

Bless this School
and all who pass through its halls of learning.
May its teachers be filled with love
and skilled in imparting true knowledge.
May its students be openminded
and welcome the teachings with joy and eagerness.
May this School always be the home of truth and wisdom,
faith and goodwill toward all,
helping to build up our community
and Your Kingdom of justice, love, and peace.
We ask this in the Name of Jesus the Lord.

## Blessing of a Workplace

HEAVENLY Father,
Lord and organizer of the universe,
you gave us the task of subduing the earth
as Your privileged coworkers (Gen 1:28).
In carrying out this task
human beings have become engaged
in all types of business,
aided by their mental and physical gifts
as well as the machines they use.

Bless this Workplace.
May all that is done here serve to enhance human life
and so contribute to a deeper spiritual life for all.
May those who work here in any manner
always act with justice and practice charity.
May they never forget that our principal business on earth
is to love and serve You
and our fellow human beings.

## Blessing of a Place of Recreation

COMPASSIONATE Lord Jesus Christ,
You bid Your disciples one day
to come apart for a while and rest (Mk 6:31).
In so doing, You taught us
that the bow should not always be bent,
but that we have a very human need
for genuine diversion, relaxation, and recreation.

Bless this Place of Recreation.
May it provide wholesome relaxation,
the kind that is good for the body
and good for the soul,
the kind that in no way leads to anything
that is offensive to You.
May all who come here attain relaxation
and return to their daily activities
better able to fulfill the tasks You have set for them.

## Blessing of a Neighborhood

LORD God,
You made us social beings
and destined us for family life in heaven.

Your Son, Who chose to die for all human beings,
told us to love our neighbor as ourselves (Mt 19:19).
All were made after Your image.
That is the reason why we now ask You
to bless our Neighbors and our Neighborhood.
May we strive to preserve loving union among us,
always ready to help one another in time of need.
May we resemble the first Christians
who after Pentecost were of one heart and one mind (Acts 4:32).

## Blessing of a Hospital

LORD God,
You are the compassionate Father of Your people,
comforting us in our afflictions
and healing our maladies.
You sent Your only Son, the Good Samaritan,
to heal our physical and spiritual sickness.
He does so by bringing us to His Church, saying:
Look after them and I will repay You
on my way back (cf. Lk 10:25ff).

Bless this Hospital that is an extension
of the Divine mercy and compassion.
May Your Spirit comfort all who come here in pain
and enable them to leave in joy.
May that same Spirit prompt all who care for the sick
to carry out their duties and ministry
in true Christian love and service,
ever mindful of the words of Jesus:

"Whatever you did
for one of the least of these brothers and sisters
of Mine,
you did for Me" (Mt 25:40).

## –3–

# Prayer-Blessings of Things — *Christifying the Universe*

THROUGH the power of Christ's saving Mystery all things in the world can be renewed and supernaturalized. Everything can be made to work for the greater glory of God and the salvation of all human beings. By a judicious use of blessings we can Christify the entire universe.

*It is rather fitting to conclude this book with the section dedicated to blessing things and bringing them into accord with the Divine redemption. The prayers found here show how we can sanctify the whole world of things, both animate and inanimate, dedicating them to the use of God's people. May we so use them as to truly restore all things in Christ.*

### Blessing of Food

HEAVENLY Father and Lord of the universe,
You are Providence and Supreme Provider,
but You desire our cooperation.
Bless those who sow, plant, water,
and ultimately bring in the harvest.
Bless all who transport our food.

May they bring wholesome nourishment
to many people.
But we do not live on bread alone (Mt 4:4).
We need food for our souls.
As we feed our bodies, may we also be concerned
about our spiritual life
and those who care for it—the harvesters of souls.
Grant this through Christ our Lord.

## Blessing of a Pet

LORD God,
You have made all living things
and You are even more wonderful
than the things You have made.
We thank You for giving us our pets
who are our friends
and who give us so much joy in life.

Bless this Pet.
May it give us joy and remind us of Your power.
May we realize that
as our pets trust us to take care of them,
so we should trust You to take care of us,
and in taking care of them
we share in Your love for all Your creatures.
Grant this through Christ our Lord.

## Blessing of an Automobile

MERCIFUL God,
automobiles transport many people every day
and there is also the threat of accidents
for those who make use of them.

Bless this Automobile.
May Your Angels guard those who use it.

May its drivers proceed carefully at a proper speed,
always conscious of their great responsibility.
And may all who reach their earthly destination in it
also enjoy a safe journey to their heavenly home.
We ask this through Christ our Lord.

## Blessing of a Boat

LORD Jesus Christ,
You are the supreme Fisherman of souls.
You frequently traveled by boat on the Lake of Gennesaret
and from a boat you sometimes preached to crowds (Mt 13:2).
You chose fishermen to be your disciples (Mk 1:16f)
and calmed the storm for their safety (Mk 4:39).

Bless this Boat.
May it always be used for good purposes,
and ever ferry its passengers to their proper port.
May it remind them of the great blessing
of belonging to the Church,
sometimes called the Bark of Peter.

## Blessing of an Airplane

ALMIGHTY Creator,
Bless this Airplane.
May it never meet with accidents,
but always provide safe, speedy, and pleasant transportation
for those who will make use of it.
May it serve at the same time to remind them

of the majesty and greatness of their Creator
Who made the sky through which they fly
and the birds whom they imitate in their flight.
We ask this through Jesus Christ our Lord.

## Blessing of a Train

LORD Jesus Christ,
how different are our ways of travel
from Yours and those of Your Apostles!
How much we have gained in comfort and also in speed!
But speed is also a cause of accidents.

Bless this Train.
May it give good service to travelers.
May the engineer always keep in mind
his great responsibility with regard to the passengers.
May he be careful and rely on Your Divine protection,
and may all who ride in them entrust themselves to You
for time and for eternity.

## Blessing of a Computer

FATHER in heaven,
Bless this Computer,
which is a product of human ingenuity,
that it may always be used for good
and not for evil,
to give life rather than death (Deut 30:15).
Let it be a wonderful source of communication between people,
a conveyor of truth not falsehood,
a promoter of the common good,

an aid to the betterment of life,
and a mark of Your Spirit in us.
We ask this in the Name of Jesus our Lord.

## Blessing of a Book

ALMIGHTY God,
You have made us in such a way
that we can learn from others
and transmit what we know to others in turn.
Books are the great instruments for imparting knowledge
as well as for forming us in truly human ways.

Bless this Book.
May all who use it grow in wisdom and grace,
and in turn communicate their knowledge to others.
We ask this through Jesus Your Son,
Whose Life was a living Book that has inspired the ages.

## Blessing of a Christmas Tree

HEAVENLY Father,
in Your goodness You did not abandon us to our sins
but sent Your only Son to redeem us (Jn 3:16f).
The birth of Jesus is a manifestation
of His great love for all human beings
as well as Your infinite compassion toward us.

Bless this Christmas Tree that we have set up
as a symbol of Christ's birth by its lights
and a symbol of our joy by its decorations.
May this remind us to accept Christ more deeply into our lives
and bring us closer to You every passing day.

ISBN 978-1-947070-49-3
90000
9 781947 070493